AMERICAN DOMESTIC VERNACULAR ARCHITECTURE

home
sweet
home

RIZZOLI
NEW YORK

Editors:
Charles W. Moore
Kathryn Smith
Peter Becker

opposite
Quilt,
Don and Faye Walters,
1980
above
House,
eastern Virginia,
18th century

AMERICAN DOMESTIC VERNACULAR ARCHITECTURE

home
sweet
home

Craft and Folk Art Museum
Los Angeles
Rizzoli
New York

Published by
Rizzoli International Publications Inc.
712 Fifth Avenue
New York, New York 10019

in cooperation with the
Craft and Folk Art Museum
5814 Wilshire Boulevard
Los Angeles, California 90036

Printed in the United States
of America

Library of Congress Catalogue
Card Number 83-616 76

ISBN 0-8478-0520-4

This publication
was underwritten by
the Ahmanson Foundation.

The preparation of
this publication was supported
by the Graham Foundation for
Advanced Studies in
the Fine Arts.

home sweet home

with a sense of place

and motion

made by children

or children grown up

of adobe

or wood

or covered with stucco

and drenched in dreams

Down the Trail
to Home Sweet Home

Ballad

by
Ernest
R.
Ball.

Composer of
Mother Machree.
Till the Sands of the Desert
Grow Cold.
Dear Little Boy of Mine.
Let the Rest of the World
Go By. Etc. Etc.

M. Witmark & Sons
NEW YORK

The preparation of this catalog was supported by a grant from the Graham Foundation for Advanced Studies in the Fine Arts.

The publication was underwritten by a grant from the Ahmanson Foundation.

We have been around the block a few times since *Home Sweet Home* was first conceived. In a project so large, change is inevitable. The original concepts articulated by Gere Kavanaugh and Charles Moore have been shaped and reshaped by a whole gamut of individuals and institutions to form a cohesive study of the history of American domestic architecture. What that might be is ably described elsewhere in this volume.

For my part I would like to express deep gratitude to all those who made the realization of this project possible. The Craft and Folk Art Museum of Los Angeles has coordinated the development of the project and has seen countless individuals labor to make the numerous components come to fruition.

For the uninitiated, *Home Sweet Home* is a series of exhibitions, a symposium, and this publication. No small feat. To our knowledge a

ACKNOWLEDGEMENTS

Patrick H. Ela
Executive Director
Craft and Folk Art Museum

project of this scope has never been attempted. Vernacular architecture is of necessity a local or regional phenomenon. To bring the various idioms together under a collective roof has been our aim.

The first "sense of place" was Gere Kavanaugh's, originator of the project four years ago. Charles Moore brought motion and wit as co-director of the program. Both have our lasting gratitude for their monumental endeavors. Blaine Mallory, Project Coordinator, deserves great praise for her tireless work in coordinating all the elements into an outstanding program as does Edith Wyle, Founder/Program Director of the Craft and Folk Art Museum, without whose support and interest we could not have gone forward.

Momentum was greatly enhanced by generous funding from the National Endowment for the Arts, National Endowment for the Humanities, Countrywide Funding Corporation, Harry Kahn, Robert Maquire and Jack Nash.

A generous grant from the Ahmanson Foundation made the publication of this volume possible. Preparation of the catalog was underwritten by a grant from the Graham Foundation for Advanced Studies in the Fine Arts. We are very grateful to both of these foundations for their support of the project. In addition, I would like to thank Rizzoli International Publications for their cooperation in the endeavor.

This volume was produced with the guidance and imagination of Co-editors Charles Moore, Kathryn Smith, and Peter Becker; thank you all. We also thank Max King, Graphic Designer, for her help and creativity. To the authors of the articles, the exhibition curators, for their encouragement and enthusiasm, our thanks.

Considerable time and effort have been given by the project advisory committee. It is difficult to identify everyone who has been involved in this capacity; the following, however, have been of great help and inspiration: Bob Easton, William Ferris, David Gebhard, Barbara Goldstein, Jody Greenwald, Thomas Hines, Ralph Knowles, Eudora Moore, David Rodes, Malcolm Watkins.

We are also indebted to the people in the participating institutions who have worked long and hard to realize the exhibitions: Jay Belloli, California Institute of Technology; Jane Bledsoe, California State University, Long Beach; Debra Burchett and Robert Smith, Los Angeles Institute of Contemporary Art; Sharon Emanuelli, Craft and Folk Art Museum; Dextra Frankel, California State University, Fullerton; Fritz Frauchiger, ARCO Center for Visual Art; James Goodwin and Murray Feldman, Pacific Design Center; Patrick Houlihan, Southwest Museum; Selma Holo, University of Southern California; Shelly Kappe, Southern California Institute of Architecture; James Volkert, Junior Arts Center; Kathy Zimmerer-McKelvie, California State University, Dominguez Hills.

Sincere appreciation is extended to Lauren Kasmer, Project Assistant, and to the staff of the Craft and Folk Art Museum whose talents helped to stage this entire program. A special thanks goes to Louise Tate, Development Consultant, for her foresight and expertise.

Finally, I wish to express gratitude to the Craft and Folk Art Museum Trustees who have generously lent time and advice to the project: Ruth and Wallace Bowman, Lloyd Cotsen, Rusty Flinton, John Fels, Mark Gallon (ex officio), Ronald Katsky, Bernard Kester, Dickinson Ross, Glenn Sakai, Edward Tuttle, and Morton Winston.

The Little Sod Shanty on the Claim.

AIR—"Old Log Cabin in the Lane."

I am looking rather seedy now while holding down
    my claim,
And my victuals are not always served the best,
And the mice play slyly 'round me, as I lay me
    down to sleep
In my little sod "shanty" on the claim,
Yet I rather like the novelty of living in this way,
Though my bill of fare is always rather tame,
But I'm happy as a clam, on this land of Uncle Sam
In my little old sod "shanty" on the claim.

CHORUS.

The hinges are of leather and the windows have no
    glass,
While the roof, it lets the howling blizzard in,
And I hear the hungry Coyote, as he sneaks up
    thro' the grass,
'Round my little old sod "shanty" on the claim.

But when I left my eastern home, so happy and so
    gay,
To try to win my way to wealth and fame,
I little thought I'd come down to burning twisted
    hay,
In my little old sod "shanty" on the claim.
My clothes are plastered o'er with dough, and I'm
    looking like a fright,
And everything is scattered round the room,
And I fear it P. T. Barnum's man should get his
    eyes on me,
He would take me from my little cabin home.

CHORUS.

I wish that some kind hearted Miss would pity on
    me take,
And extricate me from the mess I'm in.
The angel—how I'd bless her, if thus her home
    she'd make,
In my little old sod "shanty" on the claim,
And when we'd made our fortunes on these prai-
    ries of the West,
Just as happy as two bed bugs we'd remain,
And we'd forget our trials and our troubles as we
    rest,
In our little old sod "shanty" on the plain.

CHORUS.

And if heaven should smile upon us with now and
    then an heir,
To cheer our hearts with honest pride to flame,
O, then we'd be content for the years that we have
    spent
In our little old sod "shanty" on the claim.
When time enough had 'lapsed and all those little
    brats
To man and honest womanhood have grown,
It won't seem half so lonely when around us we
    shall look
And see other old sod shanties on the claim!

Photographed and published by
J. N. TEMPLEMAN, Miller, Dakota.

Home sweet home, apple pie, hot dogs, the flag, blue jeans, and log cabins give an instant picture of America. It was logical that the Craft and Folk Art Museum, with its history of presenting exhibitions and events based on the crafts and popular arts of the United States and around the world, would, in the course of time, take a reflective look at domestic vernacular architecture. Five years in the making, this series of exhibitions displays the same enthusiasm, richness, variety, and high standards of scholarship as CAFAM's previous exhibitions. It differs in scope, however; while CAFAM is presenting two exhibitions of its own, it has also served a wider role as a sponsoring institution, coordinating 14 other exhibitions on various aspects of American domestic vernacular architecture at museums and galleries throughout Los Angeles and Orange Counties. In addition, CAFAM and UCLA Extension have

organized a symposium in an attempt to define what constitutes vernacular architecture. Perhaps it may be possible to select a better word to describe the vast collection of structures, styles, and attitudes we presently call vernacular.

When the Craft and Folk Art Museum approved the idea for this project, I thought it was necessary and appropriate to have an architect as co-director. I had discussed this idea on many occasions with numerous architects and usually received the same response: it was a trite subject not worthy of such grand pursuit. Charles Moore was the only architect I found who followed through with a tremendous amount of energy put into investigation, research, and study.

Domestic buildings are the largest personal containers: they hold furniture, weaving, clothing, cooking utensils, ceremonial objects, even the "spirit." Early quilts, Shaker furniture, Pennsylvania pot-

tery, and Indian baskets and weaving have been studied prodigiously. All of these objects tell us things that are extraordinary about our country and ourselves. Studies in architecture, like most studies in the decorative arts, have generally addressed monuments, the works of known makers, or works made for court, clergy, or, more recently, captains of industry. The artifacts of the anonymous population and the dwellings of the common man were not considered important enough for scholarly investigation. In many cases, they were even despised by those whose upward financial journey prompted them to cast off shadows of a humbler past.

Until recently, only "little old ladies in tennis shoes" were looking into our domestic heritage. Thank goodness for them, for they preserved many structures which serious scholars are only now beginning to appreciate and investigate. In fact, the study of America's

FOREWORD

Gere Kavanaugh

domestic vernacular architecture is young, only about 20 years old, and in many ways is just beginning. Some claim that it began at the turn of the century with two gentlemen from Connecticut and Massachusetts[1], but it was not until the 1960s that interest in indigenous domestic structures began to grow in earnest. Up to that time, the subject had not been taught in the schools of architecture, but in such departments as folklore, anthropology, and landscape design.

It is worthwhile noting that the convulsive '60s shook up our country in a number of different ways. America experienced the raised voices of the people it had set out to educate two hundred years before suddenly refusing to be silenced. For the first time, the people's voice stopped a war or at least hastened its end. For the first time, fashion was not decreed by the couturier, but came from the clothing of the common man. Denim was ubiquitous, clothing from other lands was worn with interest, diversity, and pride. One of the most vital and lasting effects of the 1960s was the dawning realization that the public might have something of interest to say and that it might have a history of its own that was rich with interesting and important traditions and artifacts. Clearly, America's interest in vernacular architecture has followed this nascent acceptance of its pluralism. Another aspect of the '60s was a re-awakened interest in nature and ecology, which the frontier mind had seen as an adversary; coexistence with nature was now seen as a possibility. In the 1960s, all the major principles that formed the basis for interest in the indigenous American dwelling fell into place: recognition of cultural pluralism, interest in the diversity it implies, interest in nature and man's place in it, and finally, some level of desire to hear, or at least to be sensitive to, the microcosmic voice

within the whole.

I am not a scholar or historian, but one of the many voices around the country with a genuine interest in this fascinating subject. We are a small but growing group from many disciplines (mine being architectural color and interior space, folk craftsmanship, and everyday popular objects) who have the desire and capacity for learning. My own interest in an investigation of domestic American architecture gnawed at the back of my mind for many years. During the '50s, when I was studying design and architecture, the Bauhaus and the International Style were the religions of design. For someone who had grown up in the South, those styles were exciting and adventuresome. The Modern Movement had solved some problems for certain buildings, though not necessarily for all buildings, partricularly in the area of houses. Any notions of the past were completely dismissed; the future was Mies van der Rohe, and his approach to design was the only one acceptable for architectural problem-solving. But how could I forget that I had spent my childhood summers with cousins on a Delta plantation in Arkansas in a large log cabin which my uncle had built on Horseshoe Lake, just behind the levees of the Mississippi? Another memory I have is of the teepee my father built for me out of an old awning and the branches he had cut from sassafras trees on a wooded city lot. Here, on hot summer afternoons, my friends and I spent our time. That teepee reminds me of the works about shelter and space being made by some artists today, Mary Miss and Alice Aycock, in particular. As important as providing shelter, however, the teepee helped us conjure up fantasies about Indians and other exotic people in faraway places. For there was nary an Indian in this capital of the Delta—only at Cotton Carnville.

The South had, indeed a rich architectural heritage. Later on, I went to art classes in old Victorian houses (the James Lee home, for instance, of Mississippi riverboat fame, now on the National Register) that were used as schools, but had not quite achieved the status of being preserved, for the historians were only involved with Williamsburg then. Unfortunately, a great many of these early domestic buildings were destroyed, by fire or progress or upward mobility; but many survived, like the cathedrals of Europe or the minarets of the Middle East, because of their exceptional craftsmanship.

My visual Southern baggage has continued to affect my approach to design and, ultimately, this exhibition.

Whenever I travel in different parts of America, I try to find out what is unique and intriguing there. If local food and dress are different, often the housing is, too. How do people live in California as opposed to Maine, Texas, or Wisconsin? How do they respond to the land? How does the heritage of each region contribute to its flavor? Why are there no adobes in New England, or log cabins in Hawaii? We hope that a few answers to these questions will emerge from these exhibits and the symposium.

After years of thinkng about vernacular architecture, my own architectural library grew to the point where an outline began to form for the exploration of this magical area. Simultaneously, I began to find many others who shared my interest; together, we began to look at the subject.

At the moment, we are using vernacular to describe the vast conglomeration of domestic buildings in this country. We have the log cabin, the symbol of American domestic structures, splendid examples of which are the Awahnee Hotel in Yosemite and Old Faithful Lodge in Yellowstone, perhaps the

largest log cabins of all. We also have the saltboxes of New England, the sod houses of the Plains, the "dog trot" and "shotgun" houses of the South, Southwest adobes, California ranch houses, Hawaiian grass shacks, Alaskan igloos, and Indian teepees and wigwams. The subject of American Indian dwellings is a vast study in itself.

America has such a rich heritage of houses to draw upon that we must first ask ourselves how we value them. Part of our view is a bit romantic; part is sentimental; but if we examine what is deeper, what is practical, liveable, artistic, and even reassuring about these buildings, we might know ourselves better as a nation, initiate a more conscious involvement with our land, and, perhaps, even discover lost traditions (as folk and shaman cures are now providing information for medical research).

This country's present transition from an industrial to a cybernetic society, like any period of change, is one of tension, insecurity, and the questioning of values. These anxieties, which arose as well during our transition from an agrarian to an industrial society, seem always to bring with them a need to get back to the earth, or to connect in some way with the deepest tribal knowledge. In addition to this major social transition, America is now in the midst of a similarly animated though smaller scale change in architectural styles. Resistance to the authoritarian absolutes of the Bauhaus has resulted in a counter-swing of the pendulum that has created a babel of architectural voices as confused as the other view was absolute. What better moment to consider the intuitive architectural solutions derived from need and place?

All vernacular dwellings were built in response to the particular needs of people (including their religious and cultural mores) within the limitations of a given time and the demands or resources of a given region. Weather conditions, the presence or absence of water; the availability of trees, clay, or rocks; excessive cold, wind, or humidity; dry heat, swamp, or highland; the presence of enemies, human or animal, were all factors which predicated the nature of the shelter. Many early buildings hugged the earth like a bear cub's den, designed for protection against tornadoes as well as excesses of heat or cold. Ranch houses were designed for protection against enemies and the sun, with air circulation in mind; porches were added for sitting outside and as a center for observation and conviviality. Many vernacular houses represent a safe place, almost a fortress, a reflection of a basic tribal memory of the need for security, a need that modern man, beset by different enemies, feels as strongly as his forebears.

The study of indigenous buildings does not imply a desire to return to the primitive. Obviously, there are many cooking methods better than the open hearth and many ways to provide insulation better than remudding a sod house every year. Modern technology is available, and should be used. But it is the active use of the verb that should be emphasized: man must use technology, not be used by it. He should observe the lessons learned by earlier inhabitants of his land, abjure the belief that one architectural solution is the answer for all people in all places, and deny the temptation to place himself and his knowledge above the indigenous wisdom of a place. Cavalier disregard of tribal knowledge is wasteful, uneasy, probably energy consumptive, and usually unsuccessful!

Clearly, the times call for an American style for our domestic shelter. Or perhaps, because of the new appreciation for pluralism,

there may be a large number of appropriate American styles, an amalgam, like the country itself. It is interesting to note that today cost is as palpable a factor as the weather in the design of domestic dwellings. It is also a fact that the desire for mobility has become a national trait. The moblile home, either on the road or in a trailer park, must surely take its place as part of contemporary American vernacular architecture, formed as directly from the desire for low cost and mobility as the underground prairie sod house was from the threat of tornadoes. The dream of having a home of one's own is achieved via the assembly line — a perfect American solution.

Though a continuing part of the American Dream is to own one's home, we have lost many of the feelings that went into the building of our earlier homes, the joys, for instance, of helping one another, of gathering together for a common goal, of sharing a meal after a roof raising. We have lost, too, the pleasures of inheriting a house filled with treasured furnishings. But more than that, we have lost the sense of accomplishment that comes from building one's own house or from working on a house of someone else's design, tuning it up the better to suit our needs.

Modern education teaches us little about how average Americans once enriched their lives. The responses of each individual to his locale were built into the making of a home, so there was a sense not only of practicality, but of pride and personal involvement. In my own part of Los Angeles, early in the twentieth century, Charles Lummis built his house out of river stones and local timber beside an arroyo, displaying a deep appreciation for native materials that harmonize with the surroundings. Lummis, who spent a lifetime studying the cultures of American Indians, was one of those mavericks who appre-

ciated what the land was and what a close relationship with it could yield. Perhaps we may learn from people like Lummis how even tract houses can become a personal statement — a person's castle. We may discover that quality comes from a more personal relationship with our surroundings.

Lastly, in this age of Americans searching everywhere for roots and a sense of self and the ability to fit into the community at large, the study of vernacular architecture will help us to connect with the past, and so perhaps to evaluate the present better and be a part of the continuum. Until now, people have preferred to give up the past in favor of upward mobility, resulting in an economy that often demands replacement; today's artifacts are made by unseen hands (or machines), generally not made very well. We have evolved from a society of participants into one of spectators. We have given up the past for a future of homogenization and amalgamation.

We are, however, beginning to feel a sense of loss; there are signs that Americans are now trying to reconnect with their heritage. The study of diverse cultures, as manifested in their vernacular houses, is one way to make our heritage more accessible and manageable, allowing us, once again, to be participants in our own lives. Whatever one's national origins may be, the log cabin and the California missions have come to belong to all Americans. Every group of immigrants has contributed its own cultural baggage to American vernacular architecture. Viewing these structures helps us to understand each other and to accept the wonderful diversity of our nation. You can see it in the expressions of people who are touring a historical house site. Observe, on the other hand, people touring a skyscraper. One belongs to the people, the other to the faceless corporation.

The study of American vernacular housing might even help in getting back the neighborhood. The idea is much bigger than merely how these houses were built—where, what materials, by whom; for a great many of us, they are symbols of and an inspiration for the individual in today's seas of anonymity. They symbolize what many of us would like life to be and show us how to accomplish one of the most important things in life: making a home.

One of the greatest goals we could hope for from this exhibition is to establish an institute devoted to the study of American architecture that traces our history from its beginnings.[2] What better place than Los Angeles to begin?

Footnotes

1. Documentation of vernacular buildings may have begun with Norman Morrison Isham and Albert F. Brown, who made drawings of various structures in 1890 and 1895 respectively.

2. To my knowledge, there are only two architectural institutions that are addressing this problem, and they are new. The one is the Center for the Study of American Architecture at Columbia University. The other is the University of California at Berkeley, where Dell Upton will join the faculty in the fall of 1983. Upton has been one of the prime movers behind the formation of The Vernacular Architecture Forum, an offshoot of the Society of Architectural Historians. Other important figures who have contributed to this organization are: Abbott Lowell Cummings, Bill Tishler, Cary Carson, Henry Glassie, Richard Candee, and Ellen Cox.

RISING SUN TAVERN, FREDERICKSBURG, VA.

A Modern California Adobe Home.

OLD HOMESTEAD.

M-5—FIRST WHITE HOUSE OF THE CONFEDERACY, MONTGOMERY, ALA.

787. HOME OF JANE WITHERS, WESTWOOD

OLD POWDER MAGAZINE, CHARLESTON, S.

...ncetown, Cape Cod, Mass.

Upper Main Street (Residence Section), Oneida, N. Y.

...WING FLOWERS OF BIGNONIA VENUSTA,

TOLL HOUSE — WHITMAN, MASSACHUSETTS.

POST CARD

MESSAGE MAY BE WRITTEN ON THIS SIDE.

ADDRESS ONLY ON THIS SIDE.

This is where we
take a walk every
evening—before dark
of course—How is
your Wednesday
evening friend?
my Honey I forgot

Miss L. J. Romer,
161 E. 48" Street,
New York—
N. Y.

TABLE OF CONTENTS

or Covered with Stucco

and Drenched in Dreams

Conclusion/Peter Becker

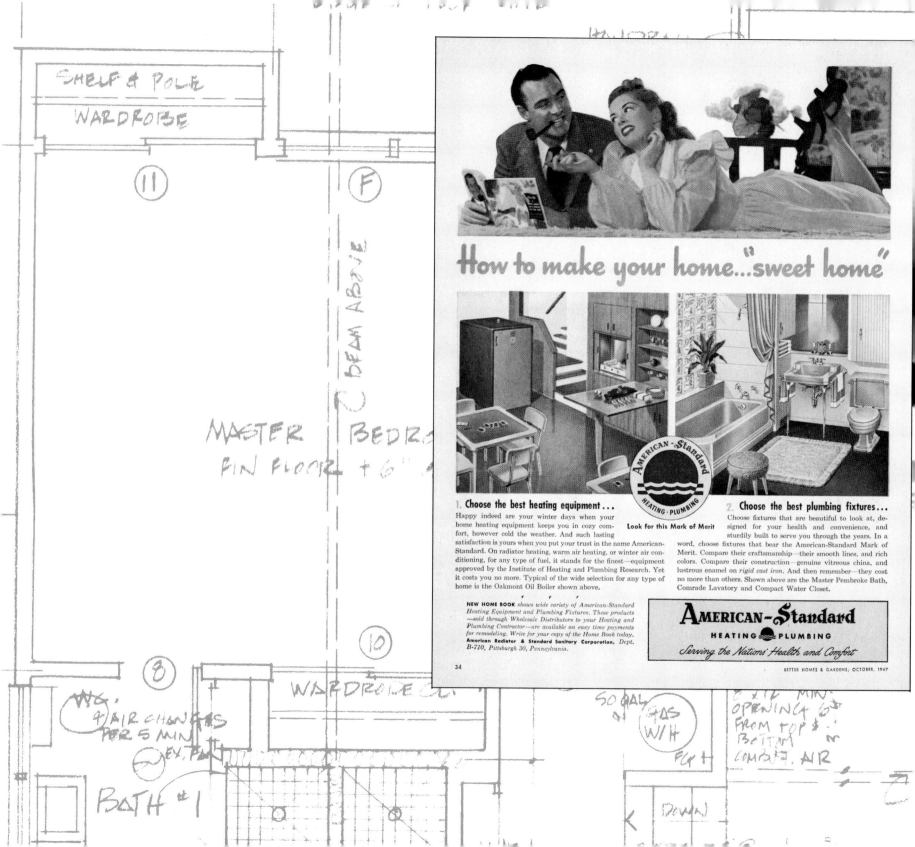

INTRODUCTION

Charles W. Moore

The word vernacular derives from the Latin *vernaculus*, itself probably from the Etruscan *verna*, which means a slave born in the house of his master,[1] a definition that is obviously not very useful for categorizing anything in North America in the years since the Civil War. So vernacular has come to mean "of the people, of ordinary people in particular"; according to Webster's, it can be a style, "of artistic or technical and especially architectural expression employing the commonest forms, materials, and decorations of a place, period, or group"; or it can be a language of that place, period, or group.[2] It is probably used most often to refer to language, with connotation of "common" that edges off towards "coarse," as when people say "to put it in the vernacular" when they are about to use an off-color word.

Vernacular architecture has less to do with intimations of coarseness, but it has for a long time remained unloved, in spite of the American democratic predilection toward it. As Bernard Rudofsky snarls defensively in the preface to his *Architecture Without Architects*, most architectural history has been written about the houses of important people, focusing on monuments and buildings made by brand name architects; it becomes "...a who's who of architects who commemorated power and wealth; an anthology of buildings of, by, and for the privileged...with never a word about the houses of lesser people."[3] Certainly, for most of history, ordinary, or vernacular, houses have been passed over or slid by; like the common crockery in them, they have been ignored by historians, and everybody else.

In very recent times, though, this historic neglect has given way to avid competition between groups, cultural anthropologists on the one hand and designers on the other, to snatch the vernacular into their respective realms. The struggle over the new found prize has resonances of the enthusiasms of Zen tea masters in Japan, who so prized the "natural" qualities of certain rough peasant pottery that they drove its price into the realm of the phenomenal. Our present-day pot-snatchers have not driven up the price of vernacular architecture, but they have come close to a curious sanctification of it: the main interest of the cultural anthropologists and their brethren, the folklorist, the cultural geographers, and the historical archaeologists, has been in the setting up of norms and typologies and categories like upright and wing and "hall and parlor" that seem to give some proper academic importance to ordinary houses because of the patterns they share. For the most part, the academics have looked for similarities and for possibilities of organizing a great deal of information about a great many buildings. Their organizational efforts reinforce the norm and narrow the definition, to reject objects that are peculiar or quirky or bear someone's personal stamp.

The interest of the architects and designers has usually been the opposite: they generally concentrate their energies on looking for peculiarities and quirks and charming examples of ingenious adaptation of materials and building techniques to the particular circumstances of a site or region. In recent years, designers have imbued vernacular architecture with most of the overtones of apple pie and motherhood, so that anonymous examples become sacred icons of freakiness. The designers spend their conferences admitting special one-of-a-kind buildings and places into the widening circle of the holy vernacular.

One of the pleasures in viewing vernacular architecture as a homely vessel become a prize, snatched back and forth by cultural anthropologists organizing studies and architects and designers discovering a rich source of inspiration is the prospect of this newfound treasure, its value enhanced, being returned to the public realm it came from. There it is as likely a candidate as any to help provide the base for the building tradition we all seem to be yearning for, so that some house-building Julia Child can find close at hand the wonder in the commonplace, the fresh taste in the collard greens, or the pleasure in those truffles snuffled out of the rich earth.

To that end this catalog describes a series of exhibits that include the anonymous and the strangely special, sometimes the work of known designers, though more often not. The continuing American attitudes, at least for the last 120 years, is not that of a slave architecture rigidly distinguished from a master architecture. Rather, throughout most of American architectural history, there are elements of the common and cheap as well as elements of fancy or fancy elements which may be seen as providing the comforting support of memory on the one hand or as unsupportable pretension on the other. This assumes, of course, that memory is considered to be legitimate and even vaguely uplifting and can be present in what we are calling vernacular architecture.

The noted commentator on American landscapes, J.B. Jackson, has made the point that vernacular architecture in Europe, especially, has never been the timeless phenomenon celebrated in Rudofsky's *Architecture Without Architects*; only after the eighteenth century or so has it even been permanent. Its ephemeral qualities are evidenced in an archaeological dig in Yorkshire where the traces of an ancient village disclose that each generation changed their house, adjusting the way they were oriented as well as what they looked like. The houses of common people everywhere, he notes, have, for much of history, been flexible and ever-changing; it is only the houses of the landlords that have embraced monumentality or even permanence. By the same token, American vernacular architecture is trendy. ("Everything's up-to-date in Kansas City, they've gone about as fer as they can go," as they sang in *Oklahoma!*) And now, of course, as images of the whole world pour in through the television sets, and people everywhere can change styles for greater fun and profit as fast as the trend-setters do in New York or Paris or London or Los Angeles or wherever, vernacular building responds to ever-quickening and, let's admit it, ever-fashionable impulses.

A part of the vernacular glory consists in rising to new occasions, as in little towns in Texas which were settled by people from Alsace or Hesse or Poland or Czechoslovakia, who made houses that were appropriate and functional, efficient responses to the conditions encountered on a new frontier. But another important part of their effort involves the recollections of the homes that they left behind, the part that makes it possible to guess almost precisely where the builders had come from. In our own time, people move around so much and there is so much high-tech help employed in building a house that it is harder to guess the precise provenance of anybody. But as fashion moves faster, it becomes easier to pinpoint the exact date of houses, 1917 or 1921 or 1932.

Another part of American vernacular architecture, perhaps in our story the most important of all, is concerned with the containment of dreams, of places and times far beyond the traditions even of the original homeland of the builder, which speak of glories from long ago and of aspirations for the future. I'm fond of recalling the exploits of my great-grandfather, a farmer who lived in a Greek Revival house that his farmer father had built on the Michigan frontier and who kept his farm books in Latin and his personal diaries in Greek. This was unusual, but my great-grandfather was not an aristocrat; he was at first a farmer, and a frontier farmer at that. Although he went farther than most Americans, maybe, in embracing the ancient past, he represents a classic instance of the efficiency of memory as an enricher of life. With very few exceptions, Americans are not peasants, attached like their forefathers to a single piece of land; we come, almost all of us, from somewhere else, and our common building, our vernacular, mixes the accents of the place with the cadences of a distant drummer.

Almost all of American vernacular architecture, it seems to me, is coming from somewhere, in the process of trickling down or welling up from someplace else. It has some relation with the past, some with the present, with trends and fashions, and with the dreams of glory sometimes classed as pretensions. American architecture, at its best, is almost always pretentious, that is pretending to grandeurs that are sometimes close and sometimes very distant. The kind of native architecture that Bernard Rudofsky eulogizes is a far cry from anything we have in this country, except maybe in the Hopi reservation. American vernacular architecture is not permanent or timeless or of the soil or built by peasants, but it is a rich combination of connection to the land and the breezes blowing through, a desire to be in step with a wondrous new place and time, and a yearning and dreaming for other places and other times that may be far away.

Footnotes

1. D.D. Simpson, *Cassell's New Latin Dictonary,* New York: Funk and Wagnells Co., 1959.

2. G. & C. Merriam Co., *Webster's Third New International Dictionary,* Springfield, Massachusetts: G. & C. Merriam Co., 1966.

3. Bernard Rudofsky, *Architecture Without Architects,* Garden City, New York: Doubleday and Co., Inc., 1964, p.3.

home
sweet
home

*a series of exhibitions
celebrating*
**American Domestic
Vernacular Architecture**

The Old World famously abounds in anciently established, historically honored places, locally or universally revered. North America has its special locations, too, with a sense of place. There are fewer than in Europe or Asia, they are generally newer, and sometimes they celebrate rites of passage (The Oregon Trail or the Cumberland Gap) or the thrill of arrival (San Francisco or Santa Fe). The pleasures of travel used to have a great deal to do with places being different from each other: not long ago, Yuma, Arizona, still had wooden sidewalks. In not many miles, a tourist could pass from a particular way of life to a very different one, each distinguished by local materials and building style. Tobacco barns, for instance, have very different details in Maryland from Kentucky or Connecticut, though the standard act of ventilating to dry the tobacco, accomplished with openings that swing sideways or hinge from the top, is always locally consistent.

In recent times, the specialness of places has faded and faded as the notion of franchise, or as Howard Johnson's has put it, "Someone you know wherever you go," has gained ascendency. People who design buildings are, part of the time, extremely interested in making shapes with universal appeal: the great Corbusian architectural revolution of the 1920s was based on the rediscovery of primal forms good anywhere — the cylinder, the sphere, the cube, the cone. But in the last 30 years or so, architects have been reconsidering the importance of singling out places for some kind of celebration of their unique existence on a planet that is becoming depressingly full of indistinguishable locations, non-places. There is the expectation that if people know where they are, what place they are in, they then have an improved chance of knowing who they are, of establishing what has lately come to be called roots. Dancers call it being centered, to feel in the middle of somewhere.

We have four exhibitions that investigate the sense of place. One looks at the front porch, at once a point of arrival and a transition from one area, outside, to another, inside. But it is a place, as well, (or it used to be) to get comfortable, to stay awhile, and survey the rest of the world. This seems a particularly opportune moment to examine porches, to see what they mean to us, before they become casualties of air-conditioning. The "Added-on Ornament" show examines five houses in Long Beach, to see how their owners have layered on a sense of place the way one might build up coats of lacquer, only here the layers contain the images and fantasies of their owners. The third show "Regional Color," relates the colors of the land and the colors people have added to amplify a sense of place across the United States, celebrating differences and the artistic visions that have filled those differences with meaning. The last piece in this group, "The Architecture Within," deals with recent works of art that reflect a special awareness of a sense of place by artists. Included are H.C. Westermann, a former carpenter who uses commonplace materials to address the human condition; Tony Berlant, who uses images of the house on an increasingly larger scale; Roland Reiss, who works with human events as "dances;" and Siah Armajani, who uses everyday objects from the house to orchestrate his involvement with the environment.
—Peter Becker

opposite
Pueblo, Taos, New Mexico, ca 1450
below, top
House, Los Angeles, California, ca 1895
below, bottom
Barn, near Libertytown, Maryland
right
Times Square, New York, New York

WITH A SENSE OF PLACE

Davida Rochlin

THE FRONT PORCH

*I needed some
  conversation to know
  what I should do
I was walking down a
  lonely street
  when I heard this
  talking chair,
So I climbed up on the
  moonlit porch
  to see what was there.
She was propped up on a
  pillow, rocking
  in — rocking chair,
Looked like she might be
  lonely — like
  she maybe had some
  words to share.
So I pulled up close and
  asked her name
  and this was her exact
  reply...*

—*Old Time Woman*
  Lyrics by Holly Near
  and Jeffrey Langley

Nobody thought much about the front porch when most Americans had them and used them. The great American front porch was just there, open and sociable, an unassigned part of the house that belonged to everyone and no one, a place for family and friends to pass the time; it was an appealing setting a shady transition between indoors and out where one could relax and sip iced tea, talk with a friend on the swing, or eat summer suppers. The informal atmosphere encouraged conversation and the easy relationships that seem such a part of traditional American life. Old folks in their rocking chairs could keep pace with what was going on in their families and on the street. Young mothers tended their babies and kept an eye on their toddlers. Passing neighbors exchanged hello's without the formality of a social call.

Anyone who owned a house could afford a porch. At its most simple, it provided rudimentary protection from the wind, sun, and rain; at its most grand, it could become a romantic open-air ballroom. Whether simple or grand, the porch connected the house with the sights and sounds and smells of the outdoors. William Faulkner in *Absalom Absalom!* describes the magic a Southern porch could conjure up:

> *It was a summer of wisteria. The twilight was full of it and the smell of his father's cigar as they sat on the front gallery after supper, while in the deep shaggy lawn below the veranda, the fireflies blew and drifted in soft random.*[1]

The word porch originates from the Greek portico, a roof with classical columns, but is now defined in American dictionaries as a covered entrance to a building — an open or enclosed room on the outside of a building.

The designs for most early porches in the United States came from the various architectural idioms that immigrants had brought with them from their homelands: the Dutch *stoop* was a small covered entrance platform with a bench at each side of the door; the English *vestibule* was a fully enclosed entrance room; the Indian *veranda*, associated with the decorative Victorian era, was more spacious than the ordinary porch; the Roman *colonade*, not necessarily attached to the main structure, was a roof with a series of columns set at regular intervals; the Greek *loggia* often overlooked an open court.

The *dog-trot*, however, is one of the few porches indigenous to the United States. Here, two portions of the house were separated by a covered passageway, open at the front and back, with access to the rooms on each side. Especially welcome during the summer, this shaded breezeway became the principal living space of the house, where many household chores were performed while the dogs trotted back and forth, and so the name.

The American front porch, whatever its persuasion, was especially prevalent in warm climates, where it could bring coolness in the summer and be used most of the year. So it is mostly in the South, particularly in its vernacular houses, that the porch has evolved into such an appealing blend of indoors and outdoors. As Lewis Allen stated in *Rural Architecture*:

> It may be remarked that no feature of the house in a southern climate can be more expressive of easy, comfortable enjoyment than a spacious veranda. The habits of southern life demand it as a place of exercise in wet weather, in the cooler seasons of the year, as well as a place of recreation and social intercourse during the fervid heats of

Comfortable Cane Seat and Back
A neat appearing, comfortable rocker equally popular for indoor or outdoor use. The woven cane seat and high back are springy, comfortable and durable. Broad, flat arms. Strong, thoroughly seasoned maple frame, long runners. Legs are braced with double stretchers. Natural varnish finish. Size of seat, 22x17 in. Height of back, 30 in. Shpg. wt., 25 lbs.
I K I L79—Cash only.............. **$4.95**

opposite
Floyd Burroughs House,
Hale County, Alabama,
ca 1930
left, top
House, near Norristown,
Georgia, ca 1900
left, bottom
House, Atlanta, Georgia
above
Advertisement, Sears,
Roebuck & Company
Catalogue, 1927

the summer. Indeed, many southern people almost live under the shade of their verandas. It is a delightful place to take their meals, to receive their visitors and friends.[2]

It is not surprising, then, that most of America's porches were perfected in the South. The largest of these is called the *colossal portico*, a porch that rises on columns for the full height of the house and runs across the full width. George Washington put what is undoubtedly the nation's most famous colossal portico on his house at Mount Vernon. Others managed even to expand on the idea, adding a second-story balcony; this became known, naturally, as the *colossal portico with insert balcony*. The *gallery*, a porch around all four sides of a house, was used extensively in New Orleans to screen the particularly oppressive sunshine. There, the house and its gallery were usually placed on top of a raised basement for protection from periodic flooding. The *two-story porch* was a double height affair with massive columns, painted white, that usually wrapped completely around a large house to create the grandest of all galleries. This kind of porch has become the quintessential image of gracious living in the ante-bellum South; Stanton Hall, a plantation house in Natchez, Mississippi, is a carefully detailed assemblage of motifs, pediments, and columns in the classical tradition.

On the crowded streets of Charleston, where the desire for air movement was in conflict with the need for privacy, houses were built with their narrow ends facing the street, the long sides opening onto gardens. The galleries, usually placed along the south and west walls, served as a transition to the garden as they modified the temperature of the house, shading it during summer but letting in the sunshine during winter. In the latter half of the

nineteenth century, ornamental cast iron for railings and screens had become available — mass-produced, ready-to-assemble, and inexpensive. So the porches and balconies of Charleston, Savannah, and other coastal Southern cities, particularly New Orleans, began to assume the lacy quality that has evoked another popular image of the South.

During the same period, architectural pattern books were advocating the use of front porches for country houses across America. In two of the most popular, *Cottage Residences* and *Architecture of Country Houses*, A.J. Downing discussed the styles, the sense of appropriateness, and the cost of a number of porches. The *Open Porch*, he said, was but a tiny addition to the front door that could be constructed inexpensively of hand hewn timber and shaded by a grapevine, though there was room enough for two seats. The *arbor*

veranda, which completely surrounded a small building, was "nothing more than an open trellis covered with grape vines planted at the base of each post."[3] The *sun room* was a glassed-in garden room positioned to capture the sun yet avoid the wind. The *screened porch* was just the opposite, designed to catch the breezes but to ward off the sun as well as the mosquitos. The *back porch*, a place most often used to dry a mop or hang laundry, was capable of a more romantic appeal, as the lyrics to an 1890s song suggest: "I loved her in the Springtime, I loved her in the Fall, but last night on the back porch, I loved her best of all."

The late nineteenth century saw the full flowering of Victorian extravagance as Queen Anne, Eastlake, and Italianate houses spread across America. Their elaborately carved brackets, corbels, scallops, and spindles were echoed in their large porches, major elements in

above
Edmonston-Alston House, Charleston, South Carolina, ca 1828
right
Stanton Hall, Natchez, Mississippi, 1853-58
far right, top and bottom
Chatillon-DeMenil House, St. Louis, Missouri, 1849

High Victorian houses and their luxuriant gardens. The employment of railings and latticework and bric-a-brac resulted in contrasts of solid and void, light and dark, open and closed. Another variation of the porch, the veranda, extended the full length of the front or wrapped around the entire house. With more prosperity and leisure time, it became crowded with rocking chairs, wicker ensembles, hammocks, and gliders.

The bungalow, from the early 1900s, was the last major type of vernacular housing to have a full front porch, a response perhaps to a national excitement over health and fresh air and a rejoining with nature. In California, where some bungalows even had *sleeping porches* off the bedrooms, the front porch became the most prominent part of the house with its gable roof, oriental latticework pediment, and brick or fieldstone piers. In recent years, however, many of these

porches have been glassed in to create additional interior space.

In the mid-twentieth century, the front porch went into a decline. Automobile noise and pollution made facing the street unappealing; instead of talking on the porch, people spent more time in their living rooms, watching television. By the 1960s, air conditioning made it no longer necessary to go outdoors to cool off or enjoy a breeze.

But the porch persisted, in reaction to new technologies and lifestyles, with new forms and purposes, as deck, balcony, or terrace. These appendages still maintained the transitional link between the indoors and outdoors but reoriented the house to the backyard as the focal point of family entertainment, with a new emphasis on privacy. Typical of the present usage is the California ranch house, usually a low one-story building that stretches across the site, with a rear porch which often acts as an outdoor corridor and functions as a circulation space.

While we may never again return to the traditional front porch, we may instead see a renaissance of porches designed to fit contemporary living. Passive solar energy design incorporates the porch as a method of insulating the home in the winter and cooling it during the summer. In multi-family dwellings it maximizes the use of limited exterior space. And as building costs continue to rise, the porch provides the increased use of low-cost semi-shelters. In the past, the porch has been adapted to each architectural style with imaginative results. The benefits of the porch, an open and inviting atmosphere connected to the outdoors, should continue to be ours.

Footnotes

1. William Faulkner, *Absalom, Absalom!*, New York: Random House, 1936, p.31.

2. Lewis Allen, *Rural Architecture*, New York: Orange Judd & Co., 1852, p.163-64.

3. Andrew Jackson Downing, *Architecture of Country Houses*, Philadelphia: Appleton & Co., 1850, p.138.

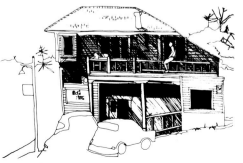

above, left
House, Nevada City, California
above, right
Apartment House, Santa Monica, California, ca 1965
left
Screened Porch, Berkeley, California
opposite
Graphic History of the American Porch, 1700-present

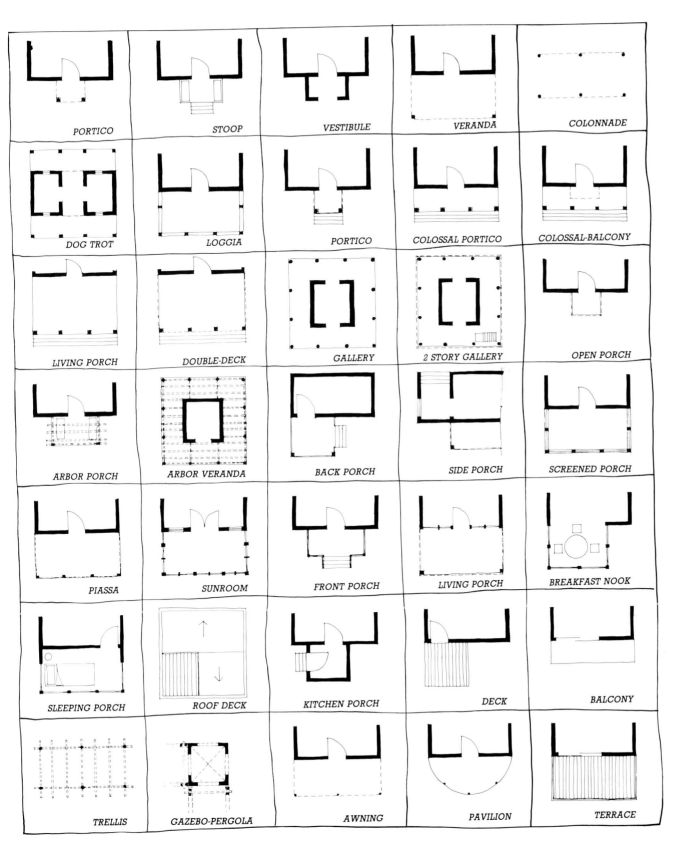

PORTICO · STOOP · VESTIBULE · VERANDA · COLONNADE

DOG TROT · LOGGIA · PORTICO · COLOSSAL PORTICO · COLOSSAL-BALCONY

LIVING PORCH · DOUBLE-DECK · GALLERY · 2 STORY GALLERY · OPEN PORCH

ARBOR PORCH · ARBOR VERANDA · BACK PORCH · SIDE PORCH · SCREENED PORCH

PIASSA · SUNROOM · FRONT PORCH · LIVING PORCH · BREAKFAST NOOK

SLEEPING PORCH · ROOF DECK · KITCHEN PORCH · DECK · BALCONY

TRELLIS · GAZEBO-PERGOLA · AWNING · PAVILION · TERRACE

Jane Bledsoe

ADDED-ON ORNAMENT

Vernacular architecture in California is characterized by its abundance of styles and the many variations on them, much like the rest of the nation, only more varied and, usually, less serious. This enthusiastic embracement of forms that recall other places and times, distant enough to seem at once romantic and venerated by history, suggests that the common man in America, a land short on history but long on romance, has been especially concerned that his house evoke something — his personality or his fantasies, his status or his ambitions, probably all of these and more.

The common man has welcomed and even demanded the latest architectural inventions insofar as they were functional ones, to make his rooms more accessible to each other or let more light into the inside or put more gadgets in his kitchen. But he preferred to think that the choosing of a style for his house, particularly after the eclectic free-for-all of the late nineteenth century, was up to him. This seemed to work out fine for most California architects, until, beginning in the 1920s, the artistic intelligentsia began to endorse the Modern movement. The common man, however, drew the line on the International style; vernacular architecture was on the rise. And if it happened that the vernacular house was not evocative enough of all the things that mattered, the common homeowner could remodel it.

Vernacular houses tend to fall into two groups: those that have continued to fit in with their owners' dreams and those that have not. The ones in the first category were left alone, except perhaps for an addition or some small functional changes. The others were altered, from the nailing on of a few shutters to a stripping down to the foundations and starting over. It is often

above
House #1, Long Beach, California, ca 1925
right
Segmental arch and columns advertisement, Architectural Record, *1921*

difficult, of course, to tell which house is in which category without extensive research but the houses that belong obviously and whole-heartedly to the second group bring the greatest satisfaction to any study of the subject.

For this study, we have chosen five houses, all near each other in Long Beach, California, to represent both types: two are in almost original condition, three have been remodelled. All were built in the 1920s or '30s, with floor plans and vernacular styles that were typical of those periods, but the various remodellings they have undergone will allow us to look at a number of other plans and styles and their variants that were popular in the years that followed. In addition to researching the construction history of each house, we have talked with each owner to discover his motives or those of the previous owner, and to get his views on the state of architecture as done by

architects today.

It is important to note that the number of different styles in vernacular houses has remained almost constant through the years, even with the dramatic increase in mass production during the 1950s and '60s, and even though every decade has enjoyed its particular favorites, such as the Spanish revivals of the 1920s. The floor plans, however, have continued to change, trailing only a few steps behind the Modern movement. The trend, in general, has been for interior spaces to flow together more, to open up to the out-of-doors, to become bigger and sunnier and whiter, and to be filled with modern conveniences. Houses of the '20s were often a series of small rooms, including one bath, a tiny kitchen with an ice box, and an enclosed back porch for a washing machine and laundry tubs. After World War II, rooms became larger, separated by fewer walls;

another bathroom may have been squeezed in, and kitchens accommodated a great many new appliances, including a refrigerator (commonplace by the late '30s) and sometimes a dishwasher. The major changes in the late 1950s and '60s were ones of scale, often prodigious leaps, which included larger and more numerous rooms and windows and the addition of the family room, to which all spaces flowed on their way out to the back patio; a four-bedroom, three-bath house with a three-car garage was not uncommon.

The first two houses have been rearranged a bit on the inside, but their 1920s facades are almost original. The first of these is an unerringly symmetrical bungalow (ca. 1925) in the American Colonial mode, with classical pillars, friezes, and pediments. The house has recently been painted blue and white to call attention to the ornament, a departure from the traditional all-

white or all-cream.

The second house, built in 1922, has been compromised by an addition at the rear, but its Spanish Colonial Revival spirit lives on in its original cream-colored stucco walls and painted blue-tile roof, expressively molded porch and chimney, arched windows, filigreed vents, and wrought iron gates and window screens.

Both of these houses have their individual personalities and charms, far beyond the range of their look-alike neighbors or the contemporary glass boxes that were to follow, but they still are not a patch on the houses that owners have remodelled so as to suit their own natures more precisely. The next three houses belong to this second category.

The inclination of the American homeowner to remodel his house, usually a house that is already the product of some free-spirited vernacular style, into a reflection of his own style of living or vision of himself is a long-enduring phenomenon, the result perhaps of the particularly American enthusiasm for independence. Exercises of the Constitutional right to turn a home into a castle, or a Greek temple, an Italian villa, a Spanish hacienda, a Japanese pagoda, or an English cottage can be found in every state of the Union, but they are especially widespread in California,

even more so in Southern California. And here, too, they seem to be more heartfelt and vigorous, more eccentric and humorous, inspired undoubtedly by the warm climate and the relaxed protocol of the California Good Life.

The freshest and most exuberant examples of American house reconstruction are most often found where the homeowner has not felt constrained by a neighborhood consensus, where his efforts could be

spontaneous and irreverent and could speak to the heart of his dreams. The most fertile environments for these creative acts tend to be in the rows of tiny houses in older working-class neighborhoods, where there are no architectural review committees and a sharp contrast to anything new is assured. These are the sorts of places where Southern California's most inspired residential artwork was born: where an old man in Santa Barbara transformed the walls of his house into frames for a thousand paintings; where an old woman in Simi Valley surrounded her house trailer with treasures from the city dump that grew into Grandma Prisbrey's Bottle Village; where Simon Rodia in Watts turned his front yard into one of America's grandest expressions of folk art.

The last three houses in our study have not reached the guide-book respectability of a Watts Towers, but they have become famous,

above
Ornamental detail,
House #3
right, top
Partial view, garden,
House #3
right, bottom
House #3, Long Beach,
California, ca 1925

at least, along their own streets. These houses, like all the other hundreds of thousands of houses in America that have been modified by their owners, can become local landmarks or embarrassments, depending on the work involved and, more important, on the views of the people who drive by.

The next house, built in 1925, has been continuously remodelled since 1955, growing considerably bigger and resembling more and more a Japanese temple: the roofs, which are surmounted by figures of the Buddha, turn up at the corners; the entry is now a set of double doors with raised paneling, surrounded by simulated stone veneer, vertical trellises, and lots of red tile. The latest addition is a careful reproduction of a Japanese temple, slightly reduced in scale, in an adjacent garden.

The next house (ca. 1920) has also become something of a temple, though this time Greek. Its classic

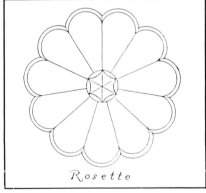

Rosette

order and symmetry are achieved by a blank front wall, relieved only by monumental doors at the center which are flanked by pilasters and then panels with a number of moldings and finials along the roof. The motif is continued into the front yard with manicured plots on each side of a central walk and with carefully placed reproductions of classical statues cast in stone. Incidentally, almost every classical detail employed here, in the facade and in

33

the approach to it, can be purchased from any number of home improvement stores in the area.

The last house, the only one in this study still owned by the person who had it built in 1935, is the most audacious and exuberant of all. In the early 1950s the owner paid a visit to the San Franciso area and returned with a quickly acquired but robust appetite for Victorian scrollwork — and enough fancy building parts from a dismantled Victorian house to satisfy it, at least for the moment. Soon afterwards, pairs of scrolled roof brackets became frames for the windows and ornaments for the gables, and one especially jubilant pair was placed like a crown upon the roof. But that was just the beginning. More and more ornament was accumulated, either antique or new or specially commissioned: a front porch was salvaged from a local house; a fence was put together out of lamp posts from Pasadena, old

panels that had been saved for just the right opportunity, and railings and uprights that are new, but look old. In the face of such a resourceful and methodical Victorian determination, the original stucco house has all but disappeared.

These five houses, covering a range of idioms as well as the full gamut from vintage preservation to stripped-to-the-foundation rebuilding, have always been the antithesis of the International style which began to dominate architecture in the '20s. That there has been a consistent group who both ignore or even disdain the avant garde is not news. Nor can this consistent use of ornament and surface embellishment be construed to have any real bearing on the evolution of Post Modernism.

Instead, what emerges is the clear statement that contemporary Americans take their housing very seriously, that they spend a lot of time, energy, and money on mak-

above
Ornamental detail,
Victorian house,
Eureka, California
right, top
House #5, Long Beach,
California, 1935
right, bottom
Ornament advertisement,
Cottages or Hints on
Economical Building,
1884

ing their "home" a distinctive, individual, and personal space, and that they are not concerned with the aesthetic ruminations of architects, artists, and critics. They "know what they like" and with joy, pride, and enthusiasm fashion their homes to please themselves.

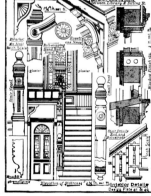

What color is the U.S.A.? It is possible to think of China as yellow, Japan as lacquer red, Ireland emerald green, France blue, Italy a sienna red, and so on. In this exhibition we have tried to explore the color composition of the United States as seen through its indigenous building materials and the color of its terrain, and, more specifically, to examine how its natural environment has affected our image of the environment we have

made.

My own interest in color grew out of the painting I did as a child, exploring and exploding the world of color in a muffin tin. Mixing colors was like magic — a visual adventure. During that same period in my childhood, I became fascinated with my mothers's thread box; as I grew more aware of thread, I developed an interest in fabric. Even to this day there is usually a sample of fabric in my wallet. Since I grew up in the South, my first awareness of local color came with each new spring. Yellow forsythia would come out very early, followed by bright yellow jonquils. Then came the beadlike redbud against a strong blue sky, with white and pink dogwood not far behind. All shades of green began to appear, spring greens of the South which I remember and miss the most. Spring's grand finale was the explosion of azaleas, of all kinds — pinks, reds, delicate pastels, and

whites. Although azaleas could be found in yards and parks, most breathtaking of all was to see them wild in a wood of oak with deep green juniper. In these places, the earth seemed to come alive. Along with the azaleas came the sweeping roll of spring winds rustling a cluster of trees and then moving on to the next. Summer in the South brought a different set of colors: crinkly crepe myrtles and powder puff mimosa in delicate shades of apricot pink blossomed with exotic fragrances that could transport the senses to China; many a highway curve was transformed by day lilies colored somewhere between Kodak yellow and butter. I began to realize the South carried its own palette of color.

Driving across this country can be like reading a book about color, only the pages are in days instead of minutes. Color in the Midwest is very different from the South; instead of red soil, vistas of farms

offer rich black earth. It was in the Midwest that I began to understand white — winter white on a bright, cold blue day, white on a gray day, white by moonlight, and white that enhanced the pines and evergreens. But it wasn't until I saw the Southwest and Southern California that I became excited about the idea of regional color. Here I saw a decided difference not only in color but in the light on color, and so began to see a different meaning in color. In the Southwest the color of the land began to have a religious signficance: the mountains of Santa Fe are called *Sangre de Cristo*, the blood of Christ. They are a light earth pink mixed with the dark green of pines and sage brush; in the late winter afternoon they become almost mystical.

California was an explosion of color for me. Southern California has a history of color that dates back to the missions and the Indian influences on them, although very

little has been recorded and much has been destroyed. There is a myth (though it may be fact) that blood was mixed into the wet plaster of adobe buildings to make them a light reddish pink. A lot more investigation is needed about Indian colors, but it is known that they were mainly cinnabar and ochre, from earth that was dug up in veins near Santa Barbara. The earliest record of mission period colors is on Mission San Gabriel's

Gere Kavanaugh

REGIONAL COLOR

top
Cactus Blue
middle, left
Pine Green
middle, right
Clamshell Gray
bottom
Bone White

northwest

southern california

lupine Blue
Salmon Pink
Evergreen
rain grey
fog white

cactus blue
Poppy orange
jacaranda Purple
sand Beige
wild mustard yellow
bottle brush red

above
Barn Red
right
Capitol White

stations of the cross, which were painted by the Indians a deep red, deep indigo blue, black, and white. Very few of California's original ranch houses remain to study, so pictures painted by artists in the early 1800s remain the best source, though not yet much explored.

Part of California's history of color concerns its continuous dialogue with light, which saturates and seems to surround every object. The famous California sunshine tends to underscore all the colors of the landscape: fuschias spill down hillsides, so intensely colored they radiate; giant boughs of bougainvillea and acres of golden California poppies dazzle the eyes; along the highways are banks of Scotch broom and field after field of wild mustard. The silver dollar eucalyptus offers one of the state's most amazing colors, a gray blue-green from afar that becomes opaline up close. The land that contains and frames all

these colors varies itself from the gold of wild grasses to a wide range of earth beiges. And the subtle color combinations in California's deserts seem infinite. As a designer, I have responded very strongly to these colors; and they continue to influence my philosophy on architectural color.

We have tried not to bring any preconceptions to this investigation, wanting, rather, to ask many questions and discover a few answers about color. Each region of America is decidedly different in terrain, flora, climate, natural resources, and cultural heritage, all of which should be considered. Some conclusions are easy to arrive at: we know, for example, that an abundance of wood contributed to the beautiful gray wood shingles of the Salt Box houses in New England. But the use of particular colors, particularly in vernacular building, is a far more complex issue. Why, for instance, are the

southwest southeast new england midwest

Blue bonnet blue
navajo white
sangre christo red
crystal Blue
turquoise blue

Daffodil yellow
Red bud Pink
Dogwood Pink
hot red clay
cotton white

Barn Red
Puritan Brown
Blueberry Blue
Pumpkin Orange
fence Brown
maple yellow

steel grey
wheat Beige
pine green
winter white
soot Black
moonlight white

window frames of houses belonging to Blacks along the Carolina Coast painted blue, while in the far West, the window frames of the Indian pueblos are turquoise? Why, in the same areas as the pueblos, were the houses of Spanish descendants painted in soft pastels? The culture and the sociological circumstances of the builders have an effect on their buildings. How do buildings in the United States that were derived from Spanish sources differ from similarly derived buildings in Mexico and South America? What palette and color sense did the early settlers from England or the slaves from Africa bring to their new environment?

In order to find answers to some of these questions, six people (including myself), who are closely involved with color, have investigated their own areas to determine the color of the environment. The evolution of regional vernacular color and its present use (or non-use) was the main concern of our study. We have taken photographs of our discoveries, collected ground and foliage samples, and matched colors with swatches. At the same time, we have researched historical and cultural influences. We have hoped to learn how color was used in the past, how people from diverse backgrounds brought their vision to the new land, and how we respond with color in our communities today. We have wanted to know the role that weather conditions have played in the use of color. In New England some of the early Puritan houses have weathered through the decades to become a silver-black, a kind of weathering that would never be found in Southern California, where wood bleaches out to a white silver-gray. And we have tried, too, to discover how the environment is perceived differently in different parts of the country.

Does a person from the Northwest look at color with different eyes than a person from the Plains? What colors are comfortable in a cold climate as opposed to a warm one?

We have also taken into account how major events of the past have affected the color on buildings. The most famous example perhaps was Nepoleon, who brought back to France a whole palette from Egypt. Technology, as well, has played a part in architectural color. In the late nineteenth century, the grinding of paint became a mechanical rather than a manual procedure, so paint became more available to the common man and, furthermore, could be distributed to him across the country by railroad. The result, in areas near the rail lines, was a profusion of color in Victorian homes. We can only begin to speculate how the computer might affect the coloring of the future.

The United States is a country of diverse cultures and varied terrain, so we have, of course, not tried to find one color that would obtain for all, though there are a great number of colors that are laden with meaning for all Americans: some of the more obvious examples are blue denim, chamois buckskin, or checkered tablecloths. We have hoped, rather, to make a few discoveries in a few parts of the country where something ordinary has become extraordinary in the eyes and hands of a person whose vision has risen a few shades above that of his peers, who just wanted to do something different, or to have an adventure, or to add another dimension to his spirit.

Dextra Frankel

THE ARCHITECTURE WITHIN

In the past decade the prevalent use of the house or architectural background as an image in art seems to reflect an awareness that a sense of place relates to more than just a setting. It encompasses psychological impact, social nuance, and cultural dialogue. Working within an area of historical and contemporary aesthetics, many of today's artists embody a presence understood by viewers through images of shared reality. Their images evoke memories of sound, smell, touch, and space, and so become a fragment of reality or a dream that is translated to the viewer's understanding of implied dwelling and architecture. These artists work within an arena of past and present cultures, making references to contemporary architecture by incorporating imagery that is narrative, sociological, psychological, or illusionistic.

In the foreword to the catalogue of the 1981 exhibition, "The Image

of the House in Contemporary Art," artist and guest curator Charmaine Locke notes:

> The prevalence of this image in recent art is an indication and visual representation of transitions occurring throughout our society. We are seeing a return to humanistic issues, a reevaluation of the personal, the experiential, as sources for art, architecture

and other activities within our culture, and a reemerging concern for the impact current acts have on our future destiny.[1]

She further suggests that "...artists are portrayers of their times." They have "...ability to sense the pulse of the ongoing stream, yet at the same time to be precursor, to offer visionary solutions...."[2]

In 1965 the noted architectural historian, David Gebhard, wrote an article in *Artforum* entitled, "Charles Moore: Architecture and the New Vernacular," in which he states:

> Almost as an answer to the Kahnian lack of concern for real *structure is the development of a third mode which is intensely involved with architecture as building. The source of inspiration for this mode is the folk vernacular of*

the twentieth century, the non-architect designed structure. The architectural language used is that of...everyday materials and the conventional way in which these materials are put together....

> One of the most forceful exponents of this new vernacularism is the...architect, Charles Moore...The apparent casualness of his buildings is

entirely due to the source of his architectural language. But once one seriously experiences these buildings it is obvious that he has simply exploited the vernacular language of the non-architect designed building in order to make a highly refined and sophisticated statement....

> If one wished to play with analogies, it could be argued that Moore's borrowing of the builder's mode is akin to the use of the found object in contemporary sculpture. In both instances the everyday object — which exists on one level — is employed as a language to make a statement on another level.[3]

In order to explore these issues further, the Art Gallery at California State University, Fullerton, has presented an exhibition entitled "The House that Art Built."[4] The works by the artists in this show have integrated the essence of environment within their imagery. Their perception of a common language, translated through a visual dialogue, reflects the idiom of vernacular architecture. Site-specific installations and those environments essential to the concept and intent of this exhibition are documented by means of a multi-image, slide and sound presentation.

At the core of this exhibition is the work of H.C. Westermann. While his craftsmanship emanated from his early work as a carpenter, his pieces embody intense emotion and vision concerning the human condition. He readdressed reality through autobiographical reference, drama, humor, and intuitive psychological associations in narrative works that incorporate commonplace materials and imagery. Prior to his death in 1981, Westermann wrote the following statement for "The Image of the House in Contemporary Art" exhibition:

As you will notice, I've designated a house I made for the last 25 years (off and on). I started using this form when it was completely foreign to people in the arts (except for a very few) and sure as hell wasn't very popular. In fact, most people thought I was nuts.

You must understand my inability to explain or even talk about the houses I have made. Perhaps they are based on a lot of things, such as the relationship between the "Houses and humanness."[5]

During an interview with sculptor Tony Berlant, it became evident that his involvement with the house image and its underlying implications is also intense.[6] In 1963 he found a birdhouse at the county dump, reinforced it, and covered it with tin. From that beginning, more focus developed, less modest in scale. In 1966 he built a "temple" around one of those pieces, leading into much larger architectural works. As their scale increased, his fantasy became one of constructing a building around the temples; between 1966 and 1968 they became buildings within buildings. To him the house is a "...totally loaded symbol."

What could be more powerful? For me it alludes not just to architecture but, more importantly, to the head. The houses always relate to the specificity of each human life, and there's the sense that the form remains the same even though the content varies. It stands for the human presence, while the rectangle in painting alludes to the convention of the window, so the house is a stage — just another kind of convention in which the perimeters of the drama are framed.

Berlant deals with content from the aspect of houses being homes that convey specific human situations, and he considers them personal fetish-like icons "...like souvenirs of my own life."

When listening to Roland Reiss discuss his own work, it is immediately apparent that his approach, too, comes from years of cumulative thought.[7] The inner drama and life scenario is his concern, and the sets which are created, such as the "Dancing Lessons" series, are variations on a theme to envelop different aspects of a single issue. The subtle nuances between each work within the series are achieved by the seemingly random juxtaposition of similar everyday elements. Proximity, color, scale, and visual cues lead the viewer over narrative paths which represent make-believe circumstances or events. It is this creation of fiction from visual imagery that enables Reiss to form content in his work.

[This creation of] fiction...was the beginning of the whole approach for me of content. When you have a fictional situation, then you really make magic. The miniatures in particular work in such a way that they become observed like games that you participate with.

...As I would reduce things in scale...I would get smaller so I could get bigger. It has something to do with the paradigm, with modeling reality. These are all ways of abstracting certain aspects of reality and working things out. That is, you begin to have some control over what is going on in the world and in your own world in particular. Part of the conceptual part of it was that you would have a kind of overview, a placement of things low so you could see the plan, see what's happening from the top as well as the sides."[8]

Inherent in the success of this work is the artist's ability to stimulate and extract personal experience from the viewer. This achievement of a sense of place or movement through time is enhanced not only by attention to minute detail but by Reiss's interest in semiology (the study of signs and codes and how information is communicated). In further discussing the development of content, Reiss notes:

...I was moving from homilies, [then] from clues to cues, [so] that these objects could be different chains of thought, different areas of thinking... not quite scenarios yet, but territories of thought that were overlaid and interlocked.... The humor that I allow is part, in a way, of bringing these ideas to the surface. ...While my work carries a heavier content load, I expect it to do its job through the form and talk to you psychologically, through the eye rather than the words...because words never explain works of visual art. ...Words [are] only a kind of surrounding — [a] support for what's going on here.

...The term "dancing lessons" really has to do with the dance of life, a very simple metaphor, that we dance under all kinds of circumstances, and when we go to the bank we do the bank dance; we go to the post office and do the post office dance. ...These [are] rituals, some of them formalizing rituals, some of them rituals in relation to work...that we all perform, choose to perform, and/or [are] compelled to perform.

...Basically, art is a very beautiful kind of fiction; it's magic made out of practically nothing, and it lives as long as the dance lives.[9]

The attainment of an architectural presence or content is within easy grasp in the works of Westermann, Berlant, and Reiss. The forms used, though juxtaposed with abstract psychological images, are either literal or archetypal. It is interesting that within the work of Jackie Ferrara, however, the imagery, although more obtuse and less overt, evokes an architectural resonance. There are no windows, columns, or absolute box-like forms, yet the interaction occurs. Pehaps one responds to the ordering or mathematical assemblage of the material, the scale or the interaction of its geometric volumes. Recently the laminated wood structures have become enlarged, enabling the negative spaces and smaller courts to form environments to be walked through and experienced.

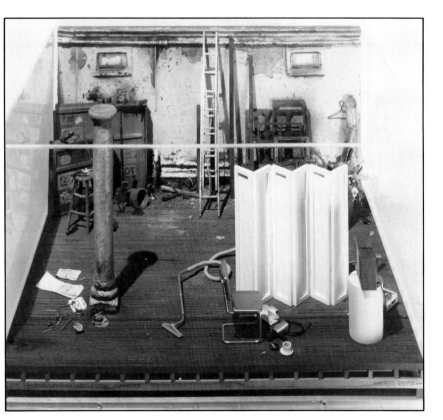

left
The Morality Plays: The Possibility of Perfection,
Roland Reiss, 1980
right
The Dancing Lesson: Reflective Surfaces,
Roland Reiss, 1980

The definition of vernacular in *Webster's New Collegiate Dictionary* is "...of or relating to, or characteristic of a period, or group; esp: of or relating to or being the common building style of a period or place." [10] Siah Armajani uses objects that seem commonplace, powerless, and casual in order to orchestrate our involvement with environment.

Armajani draws from the forms of architecture and furniture to express philosophical ideas through his art.

Public use gives the work its meaning; sculpture as location, as a place to be, as something to use. These are common values shared by architecture, sculpture and furniture. Their forms shape our surroundings and influence our activities. These disciplines need not be isolated from one another.

...The forms, materials and methods of construction are taken from early American architecture; they, in turn, hold that history and its inherent values. The house as a place of dwelling is a fundamental expression of individual freedom which is then extended to community out of need. [11]

It is the content of the works he discussed as well as those in the exhibition that allows us to evaluate the architectural setting from an alternate perspective.

...Now and in the past, most of the time the majority of people live by borrowed ideas and upon traditional accumulations, yet at every moment the fabric is being undone and a new one is woven to replace the old, while from time to time the whole pattern shakes and quivers, settling into new shapes and figures. [12]

Footnotes

1. Charmaine Locke, *The Image of the House in Contemporary Art, Exploring the Relationship of Art and Architecture to Society*, Houston: The Lawndale Annex of the University of Houston, 1981, n.p.

2. Locke, *Image*, n.p.

3. David Gebhard, "Charles Moore: Architecture and the New Vernacular," *Artforum*, vol. 3, no. 8, May 1965, p.53.

4. The title of the exhibition, "The House that Art Built," is courtesy of Michael H. Smith from his essay written for the California State University, Fullerton exhibition.

5. Locke, *Image*, n.p.

6. Interview with Tony Berlant by Dextra Frankel, Santa Monica, April 21, 1983.

7. Lecture by Roland Reiss, Santa Ana College, April 22, 1983.

8. Reiss lecture.

9. Reiss lecture.

10. *Webster's New Collegiate Dictionary*, 1977, s.v. "vernacular."

11. Julie Brown, *Siah Armajani*, Yonkers: The Hudson River Museum, 1981, n.p.

12. George Kubler, *The Shape of Time*, New Haven and London: Yale University Press, 1962, pp. 17-18.

left
Dowel, *Jackie Ferrara,* 1981
below
A Poetry Lounge, *Siah Armajani, 1982*

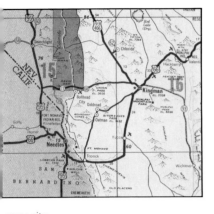

opposite
Airstream motor home
above
Road map, state of Arizona
below, top
Oregon Trail plaque, Oregon
below, bottom
Covered wagon, Utah

One of the chief excitements of the North American continent from the beginning has been not only the act of landing someplace, but the even more romantic and loaded act of moving on. Some of the most memorable places in America are not, in fact, destinations — the cities or gardens or great buildings — as they are in Europe, but the roads — the Cumberland Gap, the Oregon Trail, the Old Chisholm Trail, and Route 66. The highway image has remained strong all the way through America's history, from the first pushes away from the Atlantic Ocean to the conquest of the West and the subsequent inhabitation of it with long sleek house trailers in states like Nevada. "Go West, Young Man," American youth were once admonished, and the rites of passage to manhood reserved for Siegfried and other youthful princes in European fairy tales are commonplace in American history. The romance of setting forth is even potent to an astonishing number of modern Americans who buy a camper or a trailer when they retire or move into a mobile home community.

Moveable dwellings include houseboats, too, as well as other boats, tents, and trailers. The exhibit called "Houseboats" reveals the individuality, the eccentricity, and the specialness that that previously unrestricted life on our waterways has allowed. As Roger Scharmer examines this enterprising Bohemian phenomenon, he notes with some sadness that floating homes have come increasingly under the jurisdiction of building code people and into the conventional mainstream of American society. First the farmers fenced in the cows, and now the bureaucrats are fencing in the free spirits.

Tents are another fascinating phenomenon, found particularly useful in North Africa and in the central Arabian peninsula and, in America, more central to the life of, for instance, the Plains Indians of earlier centuries than anywhere now. The teepee, which is a conical tent of sticks and skins that can fold into a linear object to be dragged by a horse, has a proud history, both as the real thing and lately as motels and other structures built of slightly more permanent material that are based on its image.

A third moveable dwelling, the trailer or mobile home, has been an important part of the housing of lower and middle income people in the United States for several years now; it is the one single family dwelling in this nation of single family dwellings that is still affordable by the average American. Although the exhibition on trailers is part of the "Temple, Cabin, and Trailer" show at the Los Angeles Institute of Contemporary Art (which is discussed in the last chaper of this catalog), we thought it best to talk about trailers here, under the heading of Mobility.
—P.B.

AND MOTION

Roger P. Scharmer

HOUSEBOATS

The idea of living on a houseboat evokes all sorts of visual fantasies: the call of the sea, the repetitious lull of waves slapping the hull, the freedom to float off to a marvelous Walden Pond setting, colorful pennants and flags flying over the deck on a hot summer's day, the sounds of seagulls and foghorns, a canoe docked alongside for waterfront explorations, and always the image of creative, free, fun-loving inhabitants, just a little too romantic and different to live in the dull structures of land-dwellers. These images are strong and delightful, and it is this legacy of houseboat living, along with the architectural creations themselves, that continues to support the houseboat myth.

Houseboats conform easily to most definitions of domestic vernacular architecture. Adapting to unique site conditions and utilizing a wide variety of construction materials, a houseboat is individu-ally designed and constructed to fulfill the needs and desires of the houseboat builder. Perhaps, more than anything else, houseboats are low-cost housing for a talented but poor segment of society. These types of houseboats are not mass-produced, rubber-stamped commodities for residential consumption; their construction has always been resourceful. The recycling of materials is a tradition in houseboat building, including the gathering

above
Houseboat, Sausalito,
California, ca 1965
right
Gate to houseboat,
Sausalito, California,
ca 1965

left and below, top
Houseboats, Sausalito, California, ca 1965
below, bottom
Motion picture scene slate

up of found objects from the flotsam and jetsam of the waterfront to create nostalgic and nautical imagery. The largest kinds of found objects range from the hulls of lumber barges and tugboats to old sailing schooners and ferryboats. Old industrial and waterfront lands are filled with articles that have been thrown away or left behind in the rush towards profit and commercial expansion. Vast inventories of potential materials were discovered by inventive houseboat builders, who had the time to search for them. Often poor by choice and landside standards, houseboat builders had more time than money to devote to their building projects. Scavenging, bartering, hauling away, and eyeing materials for possible use became an obsession. Thus, Victorian bric-a-brac salvaged from a 1950-60s urban renewal area, industrial window sash from an old warehouse, a balustrade from a turn-of-the-

century mansion scrapped for a high-rise, a ferryboat no longer in service because of new freeway construction, and a World War II landing craft hull all found their way into the houseboat builders' collection. It is because of these found objects and recycled materials that so many colorful, floating architectural follies were created. As a result, a waterfront houseboat colony often looked more like a wrecking yard than the glossy versions of Hollywood houseboat sets. What was left behind by one houseboat builder was a new resource for another. And so the building continued, interrupted by only occasional arguments with building inspectors and clean-up-the-waterfront do-gooders. The design of the ultimate houseboat was a continuing quest.

Houseboat designers have always been perplexed by the question: Is the houseboat more like a boat or a house? Noah avoided the

problem by calling his creation neither a house, nor a boat, but an ark. Because of contemporary confusion and indecision, houseboats have spanned a broad spectrum of design solutions. Recently, in response to the chaos of haphazard waterfront development and the economic pressures on choice waterfront lands, governmental officials and code writers have come up with the term "Floating Homes." Unfortunately, "Floating Homes," located in "Floating Home Marinas," have taken on the environmental characteristics of shore-based tract houses or mobile home parks.

Houseboats traditionally have three architectural components: the hull, superstructure, and roof deck. The early houseboats of Belvedere Cove, California, illustrate this form of houseboat construction. The flat bottom of the hull permitted easy access into shallow waters, allowed beaching on shorelines

when desired, and permitted the houseboat to settle firmly and flatly; the flat bottoms prevented the listing characteristic of spinal keels and made the houseboats easier to tow. Hulls of barge form are always easier to pull than to self-propel. The need for an engine room dispensed with, the hull can be used altogether for living space. The shape of the hull determines the shape and size of the superstructure. The hull must be watertight and responsive to effects of currents, tides, winds, and storms; and it should be almost maintenance free. Drydocking, periodic inspection, and maintenance are requirements for houseboat survival, for the care of hulls is not to be forgotten: to forget is an invitation to future disaster.

The image and identity of the houseboat is conveyed in its superstructure, the space used for living and recreation. The hull, important as it is for survival, is visually dull

when compared to the strong architectural impact of the superstructure. Historically, exterior surfaces have been painted or varnished to create a watertight seal. In the 1960s and '70s, untreated exterior shingle and plywood paneled surfaces came into vogue among the more organically disposed houseboat owners. The architectural styles typified by the Sea Ranch and Handcrafted Hippie Houses have had great influence on current houseboat designs. To old-timers, these spongy, water-absorbing surfaces are considered inappropriate for maritime living.

Color is an important element of the superstructure: pastels of light yellow, green, blue, and glistening white form the traditional color palette. Architectural details for the superstructure have been taken from any number of styles, including Gothic Victorian, Swiss Chalet, Moorish Pavilion, Nautical Art Deco, Craftsman Shingle Bunga-

low, and Mississippi River Boat. Post World War II Junk might be considered another style; and somewhere there is a Post-Modern Palladian Villa now under construction.

Topping the superstructure is the roof deck. Since vertical weight is a major structural consideration, the addition of stories to the narrow houseboat hull is a difficult technical problem. The open or semi-enclosed roof deck, which often runs the full length and width of a houseboat, provides a solution for lightweight living space. Here, elevated above the water for good views and protected from the sun, winds, and foul weather by canvas or more permanent materials, is where the hedonistic side of houseboat living takes place. The roof deck of the *Loudoun*, a 130-foot houseboat, built in 1899 by the designer of the United States battleships, *Oregon* and *Indiana*, is described in *Houseboats and House-*

above, right
Ark of Noah
artist anonymous, 1982
above and right
Houseboats, Sausalito,
California, ca 1965

boating in 1905,

The great feature of Loudoun *is her one hundred and ten feet of uninterrupted deck. This is the real living room of the family. An awning lined with dark blue cloth protects from the sun and from the glare of the water. The floor is covered with rugs, and everywhere are lounges and easy chairs, luxurious with cushions, and draperies. Tables piled with magazines, and books, flowers, and palms lend a home-like and most comfortable aspect to the deck.*

The roof deck is still one of the most pleasant private retreats located on a houseboat.

The early days, when houseboats without sanitary facilities wandered the waterways or anchored in secluded coves, are over, for the solution to water pollution has

become the highest priority of recent years. Every houseboat community has had its squabbles with local governmental authorities on this issue, causing the surviving colonies to resolve their pollution problems by providing proper utility connections for water, sewer wastes, electricity, and even gas. Marinas with full facilities for houseboats can now be found throughout the country.

While early nineteenth-century houseboating was a pastime of the eastern United States, the most notable houseboat communities today are found in the West. Portland, Seattle, and the San Francisco Bay Area cities of Sausalito, Alameda, Richmond, and San Francisco all have houseboat communities. Sausalito's Waldo Point is the most colorful. Here, on waterfront lands by-passed or overlooked by developers, this free, anarchistic community of houseboat dwellers has gathered to create floating and

left and above
Houseboats, Sausalito, California, ca 1965

left
**Mailboxes, Sausalito,
California, ca 1965**
below
**Houseboats, Sausalito,
California, ca 1965**

sometimes non-floating architectural wonders. Ancient ferryboats, rotting and sinking into the bayside mud like grand old dowagers settling onto fluffy down cushions, dot the waterfront. Re-cycled components of every conceivable form and combination are integrated into floating structures. Access ways connecting one houseboat to another form pedestrian linkages that would amaze the most sophisticated site planner. This physical environment populated with independent spirits establishes a community of very diverse individuals, but there is a common bond, the shared enthusiasm for houseboat living and waterfront survival.

In the 1970s and '80s, after four decades of relatively uncontrolled development, houseboat communities are slowly being crushed into conformity. As time passes and the waterfront environment shapes up to code standards, only the old-timers will remember the good old days when architectural anarchy reigned supreme. One thing is certain: because houseboat living has always been a special environmental fantasy for Americans, this legacy will continue well into our country's future.

know that the rooms are going to be small and the finishes are not the standard ones of a house. In some states, trailers have only to pay vehicle taxes instead of residential taxes, which are considerably higher. Though financing has not been arrangeable in the past, now, increasingly, it is.

One of the most interesting things about mobile homes, perhaps because they are seen as less than houses and are not so hooked up with traditional values in people's minds, is the remarkable freedom with which they can take on dream shapes, images that mean something to people, all the way from the Airstream trailers of the '30s through the fantasies of the half century since. The Airstreams were one of the clearest visions of the powerful Buck Rogers sort of futurism that animated the 1930s, though their streamlined shapes were unjustified by the speed of the air flowing around them. But, like the

Charles W. Moore

The phenomenon of the mobile home is full of contradictions and, still, excitements. The big trailers people live in, as against the little ones that they cart around on camping vacations behind cars, get to be up to 12 feet wide, 14 feet in some states (sometimes double that if two are put together), and up to 60 or 70 feet long. There is a restriction on the height, 11½ feet, so that they can pass under bridges on the highways. They have become, in fact, so big, in spite of the restrictions to make them mobile, that the average mobile home, it is said, moves with less frequency than the average American family. They generally get to a parking place and stay there for the rest of their lives, have gardens planted around them, and sometimes get skirts and mock foundations to suggest, at one ephemeral level, their permanence; on another level, however, surely a part of their popularity is based on the image of mobili-

ty, the possibility of moving on that has excited Americans from the beginning and in some way reduces society's grip, minimizes the vision which has scared so many Americans for so long of the dwelling as manacle.

The other things that make mobile homes popular are their much lower cost compared to houses; the compromises involved are acceptable partly because the expectations are different: people

TRAILERS

roadside diners, they are the real images of their time, more potent than houses, however modernistic, of those decades. In recent years, at the other pole from Airstreams, there has come a subspecies of trailers, a sort of parallel to the houseboats, ramshackle lodgings built by counter-culture wood butchers out of recycled trucks and buses and redwood. These neo-gypsy wagons have combined, in a funky way, a kind of log cabin

left, top
Airstream trailer, Santa Barbara, California
left, center
Buck Rogers' style spaceship
left, bottom
Diner, eastern Virginia

right
*Mobile home, Rancho
Goleta, Santa Barbara,
California*
below
*Mobile home, Montevalle
Mobile Home Park,
Santa Cruz, California*

sense of frontier one-offness with vague intimations of an industrial society based on mobility. Even more interesting than the trailers themselves, which are so mobile and cheap, are the gatherings together of them; they assemble, as wagon trains once did for the night, to form places that have the appearance and many of the advantages of permanence. Today, the inhabitants of these places are offended even by the word "trailer park" and call their collections of double and even triple-wide trailers "mobile home communities" or "estates." They make elaborate use of landscaping, wood and artificial masonry veneers, clubhouses, swimming pools, and lakes to mask the underlying mobility. Most mobile home owners, in fact now buy and sell their homes in situ, in the same manner as standard houses.

One interesting case in point is Rancho Goleta, near Santa Barbara, which was developed in 1971 by

the movie star Fess Parker. It has a Spanish Colonial Revival theme with a plaster and red tile clubhouse, a masonry wall around, a swimming pool, and a lake; many of the mobile homes, the earlier ones, are fitted out with a narrow mansarded roof cap made of plastic red tile along the top in minimal homage to the Spanish Colonial Revival. The idea has not been carried through — most of the newer residences are without the tile trim —

but the luxuriant plantings along the walls and, especially, along the water's edge have managed to overcome any fly-by-night impression even better than the plastic tiles.

Another particularly interesting mobile home park is Montevalle, near Santa Cruz, which was started in 1965 as a retirement community. Those planning the community liked the picture of an old Virginia mill they saw in a Salem cigarette advertisement and sent away to that state for plans. A 40' by 90' copy of the old mill, made of wood and 90 tons of fieldstone and sited by an existing small lake, is the community center. Home sites surround it. All have been profusely landscaped — many feature Japanese Bonsai gardens — and most of the mobile homes have been elaborated well beyond their original size and style. One, for instance, is appliqued with a Greek temple, another with Mount Vernon.

A remarkably clear and orderly

framework that makes a satisfyingly stable background for the psychic mobility of trailers occurs in the Date Palm Trailer Park, almost 50 years old, in Indio, California, near Palm Springs. It is just an average trailer park (and calls itself that) with ordinary mobile homes, except that it is placed within a grove of enormous date palms, planted in precise rows. The palms alone, of course, with the moving shadows they cast in the hot desert sun, make the place splendidly tropical and exotic and the closest thing to a magic setting to be found in that part of the world. The grounds around the mobile homes are often grassy and bushy, overgrown and natural against the geometrically arranged palms and the bare mountains behind.

The powers of architecture and memory, colliding in a reminiscence of the ancient Near East, have found their way to the Arabian Gardens Mobile Home Estates, diagonally across from the Date Palm Trailer Park in Indio. Built in 1963 and then added onto in 1979, the Arabian Gardens is a lighthearted blend, achieved mostly out of concrete block and stucco, of Arabian and Egyptian motifs, though it doesn't adhere closely to either. A five-foot concrete block wall around the park employs a stepped triangle motif, vaguely pyramidal with the merest whiff of Cheops, that erupts about every 15 feet. The entrance has an archway in the center of a drive with a wrought iron gate within the arch and crossed spears above. Thick stucco-covered walls sweep down from the archway toward the sidewalk to flank a walkway and to provide bases for two gold-painted plaster sphinxes, which have been scaled down to only about two feet high. The clubhouse, with a swimming pool in front and shuffleboard courts on one side, is a rectangular plaster box with large ornaments along its

left
Mobile home, Date Palm Trailer Park,
Indio, California
below, left
Entrance sign, Date Palm Trailer park,
Indio, California
below, right
Entrance gate,
Arabian Gardens Mobile Home Estates,
Indio, California

high parapet which are versions of onion domes of Mid-Eastern mosques, either free-standing or cutout, with corners sweeping up into statements of their own. The park's rich landscaping survives, in spite of the heat.

J.B. Jackson and others have noted that trailers, more closely than anything else, embody the vernacular dream of generality, anonymity, and housing for a set of people whose individuality is not stressed. However, the possibili-ties for making trailers into strong individual statements continues to lurk in the genre and comes very near the surface in these parks: mobility in the service of a sense of place.

MY HoMe

CONSTRUCTION TOYS

opposite
Child's drawing of a house
above, top
Hill's Spelling Blocks, ca 1860
above, bottom
Kids in a treehouse
right
Children at a 4th of July parade, Warren, Vermont

Somebody once noted that no matter how cows arrange themselves on a hillside, they always look picturesque and beautifully composed. By something like the same token, children always seem to draw beautifully, to communicate directly and artistically the things they have their minds. Later, when their teachers explain to them how inept and inadequate their drawing techniques are, they turn into inartistic and frustrated adults.

We have two shows on work made by children. One is called "Buildings by the 'Little Folks,'" which is a history of early architectural construction toys in America, the kinds of toys that children put together out of various pieces to make small-scale buildings or engineering structures. These range from building blocks to miniature buildings to Erector Sets to Tinker Toys to Lincoln logs. The exhibition traces the development of toys from the days when they were unavailable or were frowned upon, to later times when they were seen as models for the work of later life, educational and character building, full of the Victorian spirit of self-improvement, and then into the twentieth century, when more and more they became just plain fun.

In the exhibition, "Rough Housing," it is expected that children will build things in the gallery, as children have for years built houses in their living rooms out of card tables, turned-over chairs, and blankets with floor lamps for tent poles. The curators and their collaborators, including the public, will observe and even participate in these activities so that there might be the chance to consider what is known already and to discover more about the spontaneous play of children. It might, this time, provide models for adult behavior.
— P.B.

MADE BY CHILDREN

**Barbara and
Arlan Coffman**

BUILDING BY THE "LITTLE FOLKS"

*Early Architctural
Construction Toys
in America*

A small interior world of color and form now came within grasp of small fingers. Color and pattern, in the flat, in the round. Shapes that lay hidden behind the appearances all about.

Here was something for invention to seize, and use to create. These "Gifts" came into the grey house in drab old Weymouth and made something live there that had never lived there before.

Frank Lloyd Wright
An Autobiography[1]

At the time of the American Revolution, another, less obvious, revolution was taking place. It had come to America at the beginning of the eighteenth century and was already both shaping and being shaped by changing domestic attitudes. This was the growing acceptance of the concept of "play" as it applied to children, accompanied by the first wave of mass-produced toys to hit the American household. Of course, most children either played with objects found around the home which they could easily transform by their imagination into a "castle" or playhouse, or they were the lucky recipients of such toys as dolls made from rags or little "people" made from whittled pieces of wood. Still, there were a growing number of children who could, when their daily chores were done, or perhaps on Sunday, bring out a toy church or Noah's Ark which had been fashioned in Nuremberg, Germany, where hand-made toys were being mass-produced for foreign markets fairly inexpensively. Although this was a far cry from seventeenth century colonial times, when just about any form of play seems to have been forbidden, especially on Sunday, it was nothing like what was going to happen as soon as Americans themselves started producing toys in quantity. That time was not far off,

and at the forefront were building toys which not only reflected changing attitudes toward education and childhood development, but would also come to reflect the major force behind American vernacular architecture, the assimilation of nineteenth century technological advances within a democratic republic that encourages new and creative ideas.[2]

The building toys in this exhibition are architectural construction toys, the kind that children put together out of various pieces in order to make a miniature building, a toy village, some form of playhouse, or an engineering structure (such as a bridge or ferris wheel), guided by a set of instructions or a teacher or solely by their imaginations. Unlike toys that are made only for amusement, construction toys are designed to allow children to learn about the world and to develop their personalities as they play. The importance of these toys, even though the child might not see it at the time, is the process of putting them together rather than any final product that may result. Compared to modern-day toys, of course, these older objects might at first appear crude or uncomplicated. They may not seem more imaginative, but for some reason the word "imagination" appears on many of the boxes they came in. They may not seem more innovative, but the term "inventor" was applied to many, if not most, of their manufacturers. They may not seem more instructive or realistic, but everything from castles to cabins was designed and constructed by the "builders of tomorrow."

To some extent, versions of these toys are still being produced today. Perhaps this is because they offer us something we believe in, or because we simply enjoy them. Perhaps, too, this is because they reflect what is at the very core of our concern for the built environ-

ment and its ability to improve the quality of our lives today; that is to say, our belief in invention and creativity, in each other, in the future, and in ourselves.

We hope this survey will offer some insight into the American ingenuity, social concern, and development of manufacturing methods that were responsible for the rise of architectural construction toys well into the twentieth century. Of course, many other types of toys

above
Kiddie Blox, 1912

gained in popularity or were desired by children throughout various periods of our history, but none were more representative of the new frontier they opened up—for children, parents, teachers, and inventor-manufacturers.

Our survey does not include many toys first manufactured after the 1940s, when plastics and lithographed tin became popular, for they, in themselves, could provide

the material for an exhibit. On the other hand, since the overriding theme of these exhibitions is vernacular architecture, we have tried to include those toys that strongly influenced, were the forerunners of, or—for younger children—performed the same function as architectural construction toys. We feel certain that most visitors, regardless of age, will be pleasantly surprised to find so much that is recognizable—for "early," when it comes to these toys, was not that long ago.

In 1693 John Locke published *Some Thoughts Concerning Education*, in which he stressed the unusual notion that learning could be at once stimulating and pleasurable. According to John Brewer, in his 1980 article "The Genesis of the Modern Toy," Locke's ideas were taken up mainly by middle-class parents and then only to varying degrees, but they heralded the birth of the toy as a plaything pe-

culiar to children and as an educational device.[3] Locke was widely read and admired both in England and the colonies. He is responsible for making popular one of the earliest education toys, the Locke (alphabet) blocks. After the War of 1812, when there was a great deal of interest by Americans in buying goods made in America, some of the first toys made by craftsmen to be sold here included similar blocks.

The first blocks to be produced in any real quantity, however, were those patented in 1858 by S.L. Hill of Williamsburg, New York: Hill's Spelling Blocks. These, and other blocks made from the middle of the nineteenth century, became known as "building blocks," because a child could learn to build structures with them and in the process might build his or her own character. They, along with Victorian building picture puzzles and "sliced (pictures of) animals," are considered to be

the forerunner of the construction toy as we know it today, and, incidentally, of the modern jigsaw puzzle.[4]

All of these toys owed much of their success to the Industrial Revolution, which made it possible for more and more toys to be produced for a vast, relatively untouched market. An anonymous writer of the 1850s put it this way, "We may not be more moral, more imaginative, nor better educated than our an-

cestors, but we have steam, gas, railways, and power-looms, whilst there are more of us, and we have more money to spend."[5] The Industrial Revolution also helped bring the construction toy into view as a means of providing a more instructive kind of play that might help a child become more responsible, and many attempts were made by enterprising manufacturers to produce toys that both parents and children would find worthwhile.

above, left
Hill's Spelling Blocks,
ca 1860
above, right
Advertisement, Sears,
Roebuck and Company
Catalogue, *1927*

One of the earliest construction toys manufactured in America was a log cabin playhouse made by the Vermont Novelty Works around 1865 and marketed by French and Wheat of New York City. Not only did this playhouse anticipate Lincoln Logs, but it also set the trend toward making blocks that fit together to make the structure more stable. One of the first to take advantage of this idea was Charles M. Crandall who, up until this time, had manufac-

tured furniture and, for a year or two, croquet sets which had become all the rage, His description of how, in 1866, he came up with one of his "greatest inventions" says a lot about how toys were made in the middle of the nineteenth century (and it is not very different from the story told in the twentieth century by A.C. Gilbert, inventor of the Erector Set):

I was working in my small factory on the then new game of croquet and conceived the idea of locking the corners of the boxes by means of grooves and tongues instead of nailing, as had been my custom. A simple machine was constructed for the purpose and in testing it, short pieces of thin wood were used.

My two infant boys were convalescing from scarlet fever, and I carried some of

the blocks home for their amusement. A house, bridge, fence and other structures were built from them. In the evening our physician called, saw and admired the blocks, and ordered a small quantity made for his own use. This was the first sale of the famous Crandall's Building Blocks.[6]

Crandall's Building Blocks sold all over the world by the tens of thousands. Late in the century, the magazine *Inventive Age* reported that they could be found "in almost every nursery in civilized nations and sets of them can today be seen in the Congo where Stanley left them as presents....".[7]

Soon after Crandall patented his blocks, other toy companies began to see the advantages of adding building blocks to their line or promoting those already being produced. One of the most prominent of

these companies was McLoughlin Brothers of New York City, founded in 1854 and widely known for its paper dolls and children's books. John McLoughlin was an engraver interested in quality printing, with emphasis on color. When a small jobbing firm, A.B. Swift Company, was bought out by a manufacturer of children's games, the McLoughlins were quick to hire Mr. Swift and market his patented wooden construction blocks in John McLoughlin's colorful boxes. With the use of special metal tongues, these blocks could be held together indefinitely—until a child wished to construct a different building. The blocks proved extremely popular, and the McLoughlin brothers went on to produce ABC building blocks, brightly colored blocks that fit inside one another, and even a toy village, complete with cardboard buildings, trees, people, and animals which could be fitted together and set up on a linen and paper lot.

After Crandall's success, another leading toy company that was inspired to make building blocks was the R. Bliss Manufacturing Company of Providence, Rhode Island, founded in 1854. Originally a fabricator of wooden screws and clamps for cabinet and piano makers, it branched out to become well-known for beautifully lithographed doll houses. By the late 1880s, however, their improved Architectural Building Blocks and toy churches could be found through-

opposite, far left
Vintage photograph of a log cabin
right, top
Crandall's Chinese Blocks, ca 1891
right, bottom
Log Cabin Playhouse, ca 1865

above, left
Castle, Ussé, France, late 15th C
above, center, top
Roman Colosseum, El Jem, Tunisia
above, center, bottom
Mission church, southern Idaho
above, right
Model Building Blocks, 1870
left
The New Pretty Village, ca 1899

out the country. The latter were made of wood covered with paper which was lithographed in a multitude of colors, like their doll houses, and could be easily constructed by placing the gables and spires on a base which could also function as the case for the parts. The Bliss Company managed to combine the excitement over construction toys with the custom in America of allowing only toys with religious themes to be brought out on Sundays. Their versions of what had become known as "Sunday Toys" or "Lord's Day Toys" included churches, Noah's arks, Star of Bethlehem ABC Blocks, and Bible Picture Blocks.

The world's most famous maker of building blocks, however, was Milton Bradley, whose company survives today as one of America's leading manufacturers of games and toys. He started his business in 1860 with the publication of games, but in his first few years he also

above
P.T. Barnum Museum Building Blocks, 1870
opposite
Richter's Anchor Stone Building Blocks Set #8, ca 1887

manufactured building blocks and a special series of unusual alphabet blocks "proportioned exactly by the rules used in making up founts of type."[8] In 1868, he attended a lecture by Elizabeth Peabody, who had, back in 1861, introduced the Kindergarten movement into the United States. This movement was based on the ideas of Friedrich Froebel, and it had been initiated in Germany around 1840 with the first kindergarten, or children's garden, a school for the instruction of young children. In 1872 Bradley put out his Kinder-Garten Alphabet and Building Blocks. By 1876, *Paradise of Childhood*, a book published by Bradley as a "Practical guide to kindergartners" received honorable mention at the Philadelphia Exposition for being the first illustrated guide to the kindergarten published in English. With both blocks and words, Bradley had succeeded in making Froebel's kindergarten immensely popular in the United States. The idea that children could learn while playing, or vice versa, was still so novel to most people that its widespread acceptance took on the demeanor almost of a revolution. Not since Locke had Americans heard such permissive ideas about education.

Froebel, however, went much further than Locke. His blocks were meant to guide the child through a world based on imagina-

tion, self-discovery, and self-development. They were called "Gifts" and were given to the child in three basic shapes: the cube, cylinder, and sphere. Later, other shapes were added according to the child's rate of motor and social development. By the turn of the century, parents and teachers throughout America were buying blocks for their children that were based on the blocks and philosophy of Friedrich Froebel. By 1930, innumerable books had been written on the importance of the kindergarten and of block building.

By then, too, teachers were developing bigger blocks to be used in schools and at home; two of these teachers, Margaret A. Trace, whose blocks were later manufactured by Milton Bradley, and Patty Smith Hill, whose blocks were manufactured by the A. Schoenhut Company, contributed greatly to the now prevalent tenet that larger blocks are helpful to the social development of children. In 1928 Margaret Trace was Supervisor of Kindergartens in Cleveland, Ohio when she wrote in *Block Building: A Practical Guide for Mothers and Teachers* that Block Building is as important in the curriculum as Music, Science, Literature, and the Arts.[9] She went on to state that by using a greater variety of sizes and shapes of blocks than Froebel's Gifts, a more practical application of his ideas could be made by both teachers and mothers. Patty Smith Hill, who was Director of the Department of Kindergarten-Primary Education at Columbia University, pointed out the benefits of large floor blocks in the physical as well as mental development of children.[10]

It is interesting to note that the views of Trace and Hill are a far cry from those of the general public at the time Milton Bradley first attended a lecture by Elizabeth Peabody. If Bradley did not invent the building block, it is safe to say that he at least did as much as anyone to invent the need for it. And yet, the emergence of the architectural construction toy probably had more to do with the ways toys in general were perceived outside the home, in the marketplace.

By the 1850s, toys were still thought of as something special. For the most part, mass-produced toys were available only in large cities; the occasional manufactured toy that a child in a small town might receive was looked upon as both novel and mystifying. To parents, these were not just meaningless trifles for keeping children busy until they could learn adult tasks; rather, children were more and more being thought of as "little folks" having their own perception of the world and needing toys that reflected the adult world on a level only they could understand—even if the toys were ultimately didactic in nature. As far as construction toys were concerned, this meant that a toy designed to reproduce buildings in miniature, for example, could—for all intents and purposes —make the child as much a builder in his or her imaginary world as adults were builders in the real world.

As the child's world was becoming more refined, the world of the American adult was beginning to expand. Victorian Americans sought culture and entertainment with an unprecedented zeal, and they began to travel great distances to attend exhibitions and world's fairs in order to see the latest fashions and inventions and advances in science. It was just a matter of time before toys began to appear at these expositions. New toys were displayed at the Crystal Palace Exhibition in London in 1851 and at the Paris Exposition of 1855; shortly afterwards they could be seen not only at expositions throughout America, but also in the first department store ever to have a toy department, Macy's of New

York City. Charles Crandall, not surprisingly, was the first toy manufacturer to demonstrate the extent of success possible in popularizing toys at exhibitions. In 1867, rather than going to a jobber or dealer, he took a set of his newly invented building blocks to P.T. Barnum's enormously popular American Museum in New York. Inez and Marshall McClintock in *Toys in America* (1961) state that Barnum "was so impressed with (the blocks') novelty and beauty that he gave them a place in the museum, where they remained on exhibition for several weeks. By this time the demand for them had been so much increased that the attention of Mr. Crandall was required at home in the invention and perfection of adequate machinery for their production. ..."[11]

By the time of the Centennial Exhibition of 1876 in Philadelphia, twenty-two toy manufacturers had petitioned to exhibit their products

—and all were accepted, including Crandall. In fact, the first major display of Froebel's "Gifts" occurred here, and one woman who discovered them in the exposition building was so excited that she immediately returned to Boston and purchased a set at Milton Bradley's store for her seven year old son, Frank. Her name was Anna Lloyd Wright. Like her, many parents soon found that exhibitions were excellent places to discover new or exotic toys.

By the turn of the century, numerous manufacturers were extolling the quality of their wares at exhibitions across the country. By far the most popular of these was the F. Ad Richter Company, which made ceramic stone building blocks. Even though the Richter Company was based in Germany, its sales were so great during the late 1800s that it opened a branch office in New York and managed to convince the Milton Bradley Com-

pany to be its American representative. Their blocks, which won gold medals at the Paris Exposition in 1900 and the St. Louis Exposition in 1904, were billed as "the toy a child loves best." They came in a variety of architectural shapes and sizes and authentic stone colors, including brick and slate, and would fit together to create amazingly realistic miniature buildings which reflected the popular Romanesque Revival style. Other manufacturers were finding that, like Crandall, they had to become increasingly inventive in order to handle their phenomenal growth in sales. The Embossing Company of Albany, New York became extremely successful in manufacturing alphabet blocks after its founder, J.W. Hyatt, invented machines that could turn out blocks at the then mindboggling rate of ninely per minute while Jesse A. Crandall of New York City (cousin to Charles M. Crandall) came up with the idea of making building blocks that could be nested within each other for easy shipping and yet, when unpacked, could be stacked to form a pyramid over three feet tall!

As Americans entered the twentieth century, they came to appreciate the world's achievements in science and engineering which seemed about to usher in a brighter future, and their toys mirrored that optimism. The Eiffel Tower, built for the Paris Universal Exposition in 1889, and the proud and elegant steel framed Wainwright Building of St. Louis in 1891, one of the first modern skyscrapers, became symbols of what mankind could accomplish, and they served as challenges to the imaginations of toy inventors and manufacturers on both sides of the Atlantic. By 1900, Frank Hornby in England had come up with the first articulated framework construction toy, Mechanics Made Easy, later shortened to Meccano. Consisting of metal slats with equidistant holes, it could be used to build models of almost any type of engineering project — from iron bridges to the Eiffel Tower. By 1904, the American Art Stone and Manufacturing Company of Cleveland had added tiny "steel" beams to their sets of stone blocks so that children could make miniature skyscrapers.

And by 1909, A.C. Gilbert of Connecticut had hit upon an idea that was about to transform the very future of the American toy industry: in a construction set similar to Meccano, which he merely hoped to sell door-to-door along with his successful "Mysto-Magic" sets, Gilbert offered for the first time gears, pinions, an electric motor, and more realistic looking girders. He called his invention the Mysto-Erector (later shortened to Erector), and it rapidly became one of the most sought after toys in the world. Yet the idea came about simply, according to Gilbert, while commuting by train between New Haven and New York, looking out the window at the girders of the New Haven Railroad's electrification program. He then spent more than a year putting his metal strips, nuts and bolts, and gears into various configurations before he considered the set ready for patent. Today, the Erector Set is considered the oldest mass-produced toy on the market.

The second-oldest, however, was developed not long after the Erec-

tor Set, and it too was a construction toy. In 1914, Charles Pajeau took out a patent for "Toy Construction Blocks" after watching children play with sticks and spools; since then children across the nation have played with the sticks and round connecting links made famous by Pajeau's company, the Toy Tinkers of Evanston, Illinois. Though not complex enough to build many realistic structures, Tinkertoys have nevertheless provided even the very young child with seemingly limitless construction possiblilties. With but one exception, Tinkertoy is perhaps the last notable construction toy to be a product of the age of building with structural steel; that one exception was a set marketed under the name Bilt-E-Z by Scott Manufacturing Company of Chicago in the 1920s. It did not take the world by storm; however, for at least a decade, children were putting together its unique metal facades to

build whole cities of "proud and elegant" skyscrapers.

Now, in looking back, it is difficult for us to fully comprehend the impact of these toys on previous generations. But they have become symbols of our past, and whether or not we have played with similar toys, they help us to better understand ourselves and our time. If it seems that many toys today do no more that keep children busy without granting anything in return, their counterparts can also be found in certain Victorian toys that were sold only for amusement. But if it appears that the half-dozen or more toys our children receive each year at Christmas time alone are appreciated only for a short time before they seem to disappear, then perhaps we should take a closer look at what is expected of them. Even when just prior to the end of the nineteenth century, Montgomery Ward and Sears-Roebuck

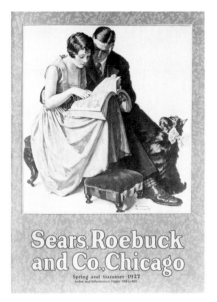

Sears, Roebuck and Co. Chicago
Spring and Summer 1927
Index and Information Pages 550 to 570

opposite, left
Girder bridge, Wyoming
right
*Mysto Erector Set #3,
1912*
above
*Cover, Sears, Roebuck
and Company Catalogue,
1927*
right
*Advertisement, Sears,
Roebuck and Company
Catalogue, 1927*

61

catalogs made it possible for children in remote farming areas of the country to have the same toys as children in the city, manufactured toys were wtill highly revered, and architectural construction toys, in particular, were considered extraordinary. As *Playthings* magazine pointed out in 1903, on the average, each child in America received two toys a year.[12] Yet, there was a good chance that one of them would be a building toy, either because of its instructional value or because the inventor-manufacturers admired their products as much as those who bought them; the creativity and craftsmanship that went into producing something that could have endless construction possibilities became part of its appeal.

If some underlying reason can be found for the prevalence of building toys, it may well be that they mirrored values shared by both the parents and the manufacturers, values which were tied to the child's development as a person; namely, the sense of personal worth gained in constructing something, the human awareness and identification necessary to bring that construction to life, and the feeling of responsibility necessary to take apart and re-box the various pieces for future use. Even the now familiar Lincoln Logs, which were invented by John Lloyd Wright (Frank Lloyd Wright's son) in 1918, fostered these values. Packaged in colorful boxes with a simple drawing on the front (rather than a photograph of children playing with logs), they required special care to repack and came in a much greater variety of sizes than today's version. This made it necessary for the child to actually "work out" beforehand what was to be built or to take courage and so develop a simple structural system through trial and error. In this latter case, the child had to overcome numerous difficulties to obtain a working

knowledge of balance and proportion, in much the same way as building designers overcame more complex problems in the adult world. In this way the child became, again, one of the "little folks."

Perhaps it is courage, though, for adults as well as children, that this exhibit is most about: courage to play, courage to learn, courage to investigate, and courage to discover. We hope that visitors might find all of these possibilities here and have fun doing it. We hope, also, that they might find, in words taken from the cover of Lincoln Logs, "interesting playthings typifying 'the spirit of America.'"

Footnotes

1. Frank Lloyd Wright, *An Autobiography*, New York: Longmans, Green and Co., 1932, p.34.

2. John A. Kouwenhoven, *Made in America, The Arts in Modern Civilization*, Garden City, New York: Doubleday & Co., 1948, pp.15-16.

3. John Brewer, "Childhood Revisited: The Genesis of the Modern Toy," *History Today*, December, 1980, pp.32-39.

4. Gwen White, *Antique Toys and Their Background*, New York: Arco Publishing Co., Inc., 1971, p.141.

5. George Savage, *A Concise History of Interior Decoration*, New York: Grosset & Dunlap Publishers, 1966, p.232.

6. Inez and Marshall McClintock, *Toys in America*, Washington, D.C.: Public Affairs Press, 1961, pp.156-157.

7. McClintock, *Toys*, p.158.

8. McClintock, *Toys*, p. 262.

9. Margaret Trace, *Block Building: A Practical Guide for Mothers and Teachers*, Springfield, Mass.: Milton Bradley Co., 1928, *vii*.

10. Ruth and Larry Freeman, *Cavalcade of Toys*, New York: Century House, 1942, p.345.

11. McClintock, *Toys,* p.157.

12. McClintick, *Toys,* p.368.

Bibliography

American Institute of Architects Foundation. *Just For Fun! A Celebration of Architecture*. Exhibition Catalog for the Octagon. Xeroxed. Washington, D.C.: American Institute of Architects Foundation, April 1979.

Barenholtz, Bernard and McClintock, Inez. *American Antique Toys 1830-1900*. New York: Harry N. Abrams, Inc., 1980.

Bowen, H. Courthope. *Froebel and Education through Self-Activity*. New York: Charles Scribner's Sons, 1894.

Daiken, Leslie. *World of Toys*. London: Lambarde Press, 1963.

Foley, Dan. *Toys through the Ages*. Philadelphia: Chilton Co., 1962.

Fraser, Antonia. *A History of Toys*. New York: Delacorte Press, 1966.

Froebel, Friedrich. *The Education of Man*. Translated by W.N. Hailmann, A.M. New York: D. Appleton and Co., 1887.

Gordon, Lesley. *Peepshow into Paradise*. New York: John De Graff, Inc., 1953.

Hertz, Louis H. *The Handbook of Old American Toys*. Wethersfield, Conn.: Mark Haber & Co., 1947.

Hillier, Mary. *Pageant of Toys*. New York: Taplinger Publishing Co., 1965.

Ketchum, Jr., William C. *Toys and Games*. Washington, D.C.: Smithsonian Institute, 1981.

Manson, Grant. "Wright in the Nursery: The Influence of Froebel Education on the Work of Frank Lloyd Wright," *Architectural Review*, June 1953, pp.349-351.

MacCormac, Richard C. "The Anatomy of Wright's Aesthetic," *Architectural Review*, February 1968, pp.143-146.

Scully, Vincent. *American Architecture and Urbanism*. New York: Praeger Publishers, 1969.

Whitton, Blair, ed. *Bliss Toys and Dollhouses*. New York: Dover Publications, Inc., 1979.

Wiebe, Edward. *Paradise of Childhood: A Practical Guide to Kindergartners*. Edited by Milton Bradley. Springfield, Mass.: Milton Bradley Co., 1907.

below
**Lincoln Logs,
Combination Set, 1920**

The Development of Rough Housing. The Junior Arts Center Gallery is devoted to developing exhibitions that promote children's investigation of the visual arts; it has presented the exhibition, *Rough Housing*, so that children and adults can explore a variety of familiar building materials and processes. Traditionally, museums have concerned themselves with objects — their preservation, conservation, exhibition, and interpretation, often

in that order. In recent years, however, the emphasis has been placed on the last two functions, exhibition and interpretation. This subtle shift has had far-reaching implications for the relationship of the museum to its public. A museum's concern must now extend well beyond the maintenance of the object to the relationship of that object to the museum visitor. Museums are beginning to look at visitor involvement as crucial to their vitality; this

idea has given rise to a wide range of participatory and children's museums. The definition of participation, especially regarding children, has often meant physical involvement and "learning by doing." The Junior Arts Center endorses this and goes a step further, defining participation to include the museum environment and a wide specturm of learning activities.

The initial idea for an exhibition about the role of the child in American vernacular architecture was to present a survey of the types of housing with which children have contact — birdhouses, dog houses, tree houses, or doll houses. This would present an adult's notion of a child's involvement with architectural space, an expected curatorial response. Later discussions between the curator and educator, however, centered on actively relating the objects to children's awareness of space. At this point, the traditional conflict of object versus participation became more apparent, indeed, pivotal in the exhibition's development. We began to question the relatedness of the objects to the child's own experience and found that this contact is only a portion of children's spatial play.

The result of this curator-educator dialogue was a dramatic shift in the focus of the exhibition. *Rough Housing* became a process, specifically, the series of changes children go through in their development of spatial awareness. All

notions of using archival objects to force a relationship were dropped; what emerged was an exhibition that traces children's building sense from the ages, approximately, of three to twelve years.

It occurred to us that there may be a pattern in the way that children approach building. Discussions broke into four areas:

1) The most elementary is the capturing of space. Play is life-sized and spatially confined. Perhaps the classic example of this early activity is a sheet thrown over a card table.

2) Play continues life-sized, but begins to incorporate areas around the building — "gardens," "walls," etc. The constructed areas remain as sets for improvisational drama.

3) With more attention to detail, children imagine themselves in miniature scenes. They become the omniscient controller/observer in smaller-than-life drama.

4) Finally, children develop a systems approach to building. That is, units are added to build a treehouse/clubhouse, for example, that becomes more that the sum of their parts. Obviously this development is not linear or chronological, but reflects stages in which play can be divided. These stages, and not a curatorially imposed structure, became the focus of the exhibition.

It was decided to highlight each of these stages in four two-week exhibitions. The gallery would pro-

The Development of Rough Housing
James Volkert

A Focus of the Process
Nancy Walch

Chairs, Boxes, Sheets and Tree Houses: Children's Spontaneous Architecture
Roger A. Hart

ROUGH HOUSING

vide an environment for continuous change within the developmental stages.

Beginning with the early concept of capturing space, the gallery and its staff have attempted to facilitate a child's private play. With 30 cardtables, 50 sheets, clotheslines, clothespins, and T.V. trays, which we have supplied, children will be free to create a growing tent city of chambers and passageways.

After two weeks, boxes will take the place of tents, allowing for both interior and exterior spaces. This environment will be capable of daily change as each new group of children approach the environment.

The third two-week component changes from life-sized to smaller that life-sized. By bringing in sand, clay, and other malleable materials, we hope to encourage children's imaginary adventures into micro-worlds. Children will be free to map and add detail, creating a changing miniature environment that 'fills the gallery.

The final two-week exhibition segment presents the visitor with a building system of interdependent units. This system, which is based on a 20-foot tree with a series of holes bored into it, includes planks, pegs, and mallets to facilitate co-operative efforts in the building of a continually growing treehouse inside the gallery.

The exhibition is not intended to serve as a play laboratory nor is it to be a confirmation of the proper developmental cycle of a child's spatial and architectural understanding. A museum may not be the best forum for such research. But we believe our exhibition does make two points. First, visitor participation within a musuem setting can include the creation of and adjustments to the exhibition itself. Second, children's awareness of architectural space is both important and natural.

The role the Junior Arts Center

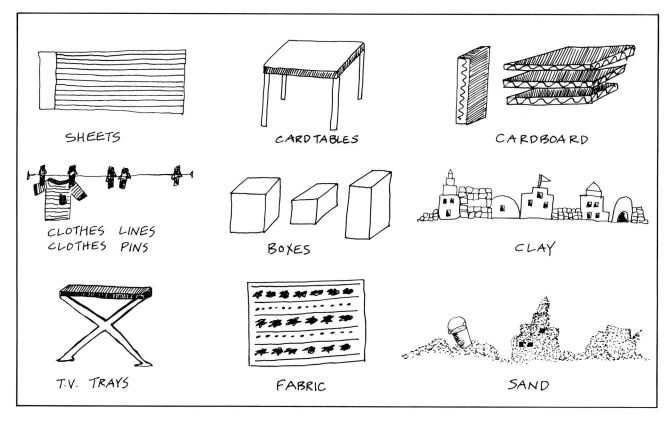

SHEETS   CARD TABLES   CARDBOARD

CLOTHES LINES
CLOTHES PINS   BOXES   CLAY

T.V. TRAYS   FABRIC   SAND

Gallery has chosen with this exhibition can set the boundaries within which children create magical worlds.

A Focus on the Process. This article explores the philosophical and educational foundation upon which the exhibit, *Rough Housing*, is based. *Rough Housing* is a participatory exhibit concerned primarily with children's vernacular architecture — a type of architecture which is largely process-oriented. It is a process we know very little about and yet one that seems to have great significance for children throughout various stages of their personal growth and development. In attempting to explore this unknown territory, the exhibit offers more questions than answers: What is this process? What forms will it take? What impact will the exhibit have on participants and viewers? We hope that some of these questions will be answered by simply watching the children.

Children's Vernacular Architecture: What is it? Perhaps the best way to define children's vernacular architecture is to invite you to reminisce. For many of us the birth of our fantasies and of our imaginative and creative abilities took place in secret hiding places that we built with such household items as sheets, pillows, chairs, or boxes. It is this type of play, this spontaneous untaught building process of exploring objects and creating fantasy worlds, that we define as children's vernacular architecture.

Unlike most of the exhibits on vernacular architecture which display objects or products (e.g., photographs of log cabins), in children's vernacular architecture it is the process of building that appears most important. Many of the structures built by children are temporary. At different stages of child development the type of activity and the choice of materials varies. Moreover, at times, it appears that taking things apart and re-arranging the parts is more significant than construction.

As one might also remember from childhood, or from observing one's own children, this type of play is often a clandestine one, carried out in places that are hidden, intentionally separate from parents and the outside world. As privacy and secrecy seem to be so inherent, there are many aspects of the process that will perhaps remain a mystery. We hope that by using still and video cameras, and having the children make diaries, some of this hidden activity will reveal itself.

Those of us who are parents, particularly of toddlers, are familiar with what this process looks like from the outside. At times, it looks more like a house in chaos than a creative developmental phase. Sometimes this imaginative play, building, and social interaction take place on vacant lots, sometimes in playrooms, or, of course, in forbidden territory, such as a living room. We hope that by reading this article and participating in the exhibit, parents and teachers will be reminded of their own childhood adventures in building and of the important role these activities played in forming perceptions and a sense of place in the world.

The Evolution of Rough Housing: From Objects to Process. By presenting *Rough Houseing* as a participatory exhibition, the Junior Arts Center provides the opportunity for children to work with a wide variety of materials and encourages adults to take part as well, as observers or as resources for the children. It might seem odd that a gallery would choose to exhibit children building structures, since we are accustomed as curators, educators, or gallery visitors to working with and looking at objects.[1] We hope, however, that our presentation of this process for observation in a gallery setting, along with films, slides, and additional resource materials, will encourage visitors to think of the vernacular architecture of children as an important and essential part of their creative growth.

The Role of Education: A Delicate Balance. The exhibition is designed to offer visitors an experience that will not only explore, but foster building instincts, creative decision making, problem solving, and, among other things, social interaction. The key is to stretch the imaginative and creative abilities of the participants without intervening or inhibiting the process.

In addition to providing the opportunity for children to exercise building instincts, gallery educators and parents will serve as resources for challenging and aiding these activities. This is a somewhat controversial aspect of the exhibit that will have to be watched continually and probably modified as the exhibit progresses. On the one hand, children's vernacular architecture implies that the children should be set free with no guidance from outsiders. On the other hand, seeking answers from adults is a very natural part of a child's play and exploration. The point, then, is not to intervene, but to create a supportive environment with educators and adult visitors acting as resources when problems or questions arise.

Gallery educators will orient visitors to the nature of the exhibit and the materials available, help children to work in groups, and stimulate their group decision making and problem solving. Mounted photographs of other forms of American vernacular architecture will be available as a resource for problem solving. So, in addition to encouraging children to build, we are teaching them by direct experience to explore available resources and options when they make creative decisions. Finally, we can help children exercise this type of play by suggesting where it can take place beyond the Junior Arts Center Gallery — a backyard, closet, playroom, or vacant lot down the street — places that are not threatening to adult social values yet permit full freedom of activity and imagination.

Films and slides of other structures built by children will be shown in a separate area of the gallery to promote awareness of

children's vernacular architecture on a broader scale. The slides and video tapes will document and provide an overview of the various structures being built in the *Rough Housing* exhibit. In addition to working with individual visitors and school tours, we will offer weekend workshops that will allow teachers and parents to meet with people who are knowledgeable about children's spontaneous architecture while their children work in the

PRODUCT vs *process*

gallery.

Because so little is known about children's vernacular architecture, the Junior Arts Center Gallery has set up this exhibit to ask questions, to allow for observation, and to explore and foster an increasing awareness of children's spontaneous architecture as a necessary and vital activity.

Chairs, Boxes, Sheets and Tree Houses: Children's Spontaneous Architecture. Children create places for themselves from at least the age of three and probably earlier. It is, however, often difficult to identify children's earliest places, for they are "found" rather than built. Even though these early found places are imaginary rather than physical and are of the most primitive kind, they are selected from a large universe of objects and are transformed from their adult function, such as a table for eating, to a place for the child, so they sure

ly must be thought of as architecture — the art of creating places for human use. Because these transformations are imagined, we cannot know how early this kind of architecture begins. Although my observations have been primarily in the U.S.A., particularly in a New England town,[1] children's architecture seems to be as universal a phenomenon as adult architecture. We might surmise that the making of places to be in is one of a small set of archetypical human behaviors with important survival value for a culture and developmental advantages for individual children.[2] It is difficult to predict the age at which most children will make certain types of buildings, for each type is strongly influenced by the available materials, which vary dramatically according to climate and vegetation and various cultural practices around the world. It is possible, however, to identify an approximate developmental se-

quence for children in North America.

The early architectural places of North American children are generally "found" beneath chairs and tables and under sheets or out-of-doors in bushes and boxes and piles of dried leaves. It is but a single jump from this imaginary architecture to the act of building, the movement and combination of these everday objects to make new kinds of spaces. In almost every instance, even with young children, the making of this architecture is cooperative, as described by Susan Isaacs in her observations of children making "cozy places" in her school.[3] As children grow older they become less satisfied with simple spaces where all of the parts and furnishings are imagined. Children of eight years and older more often make serious attempts to build physical structures.

Site Qualities and Material Preferred by Children. More im-

portant than the different materials are the different attitudes held by parents and other child caretakers regarding the use of these materials. Though materials and attitudes often go hand-in-hand: manicured gardens and yards are usually highly controlled by adults; the ones with long grass, untrimmed bushes, trees, and numerous odds and ends lying around are often places where children are allowed more freedom. Many new suburban housing tracts are of the first category, where the landscape elements most important to children have been systematically removed. Parents who think they need a manicured garden should think, as well, of their children's needs by leaving some areas undefined, unless there is a common wildland nearby.

Snow, where it falls, can erase many of the constraints caused by adult domination of the landscape and, by itself, is a wonderful

material with which children can exercise their skills as architect. *Nanook of the North*, the famous film by Robert Flaherty, showed us how quickly and effectively a young eskimo can build with it. In New England, I have observed children under even eight years of age create roofed structures by digging tunnels in the snow.

Small-scale Architecture. Apart from making full-sized architecture, children spend a great deal of time building miniature places out of dirt, sand, and blocks. The materials provided for a child's micro-modelling of the environment make a difference. Bernard Rudofsky has argued that a reliance upon building blocks in the early school years tends to teach children reductionism.[4] Others, however, have expounded upon the creative values of blocks.[5] One type of material that certainly does not foster reductionism is sand. When water is available, the potential of sand for creative architecture is unlimited. Furthermore, this medium seems to be particularly effective in encouraging cooperative play between children.

Some Psychological and Social Benefits of Building. No single theory about child play can do justice to the rich diversity and multiple benefits of children's play,[6] so I will now review some of the most relevant current theories to support what ought to be obvious simply by observing how children choose their activities during free play: freedom of opportunity to build holds important values for their development.

First, it is worthwhile to note that one of the special qualities of the physical environment is that it remains stable. Children come to know themselves through their transactions with both the physical and the social worlds. Unlike people, the physical world does not change in response to a child's actions but simply reflects his

manipulations, so it offers a particularly valuable domain for developing his sense of competence. It has been demonstrated that children build places more for the joy and challenge of building than for their potential use; other children may even be allowed free use of these places, as long as they give overt recognition to the builders for having constructed them. It seems that children need to see themselves and be seen by others as

competent individuals. Consequently, arguments over the use of places seem to arise only when there is a doubt about who the builder was or when there is a failure to recognize him.

Susan Isaacs, one of those rare educators who recognized the value in detailed observations of children's activities, offers a psychoanalytic interpretation for the love young children have for "cozy places."[7] She explains that there is

frequently a defensive element to their play. Upturned chairs and tables are used "so that nobody can look in," "to keep us warm," "to keep the tigers out," or "to keep out the foxes." Even when there are no explicitly imagined enemies outside, it is clear, Isaccs adds, that the feeling of being warm and safe inside these places is of central importance. Anyone coming inside, child or adult, is treated in a friendly, affectionate manner. By being inside, children make themselves not only warm and safe, but loving and good. From here, however, Isaacs takes a massive psychoanalytic leap in her interpretation:

> The whole situation indeed represented a good mother with her good children inside her, all safe and all loving... All the bad feelings and intentions are projected onto the

father who is the enemy, the 'tiger,' the 'fox,' and kept outside. The child says in his behavior,...if I am inside my mommy, I don't have to do anything bad to her to make her give me what I want. I only have to be there and everything is given to me.[8]

While these kinds of direct links to deep unconscious feelings might play a part in the making of cozy places, this explanation is too simplistic and deterministic; rooms are not just wombs. To deal with the complexity of his environment, a child has to order it and give it meaning. The creation of safe or "sacred" places from which to explore the dangerous or "profane" world beyond seems, intuitively, to be one basic way of establishing order.[9] It supports the idea of home-making as an archetypical kind of activity in humans, and hence in children.[10]

One of the better-known theories stresses the value of play in learning adult roles. By building models of adult settings children can experiment with roles such as mothers, fathers, cooks, house builders, and architects. Younger boys as well as girls engage in highly imaginative house play. Boys older than about seven years rarely do so, although they do continue to act out imaginative dramas on their dirt-built model scenes.

Undoubtedly, the reason for these differences lies in the heavily socialized attitude that interior environments are the domain of women and hence of girls and exterior environments are for boys. Dramatic play in these circumstances allows, for girls and boys alike, the opportunity to act out real-life situations, express personal needs, explore solutions, and even to experiment in the reversal of roles.

A major benefit of architectural building by children is that it is almost always a cooperative venture. While people vary in their particular abilities, there is room in every child to discover new and otherwise unused abilities which not only contribute to a group product, but would not otherwise be exercised in individual creative enterprises.[11]

An Experiment in Children's Spontaneous Architecture. A few people have systematically investigated children's spontaneous architecture by designing experiments, some of which involve children's manipulation of objects. One of these is described here.[12]

In order to "form a conception of living space," an architect and a social psychologist collaborated in a series of fascinating experiments that involved entire classes of school children.[13] The two investigators made numerous primary forms out of polyurethane foam, in four different sizes and shapes, which could be used by the children for constructing surfaces that were flat, octagonal, or curved. In each experiment, the children, assembled in a council, would vote whenever a choice had to be made. The experiments involved children aged eight to fourteen, in regular school classes and in one "slow class" with "character" or "retardation" problems, which were generally related to difficult socio-familial situations. The investigators not only observed the building process, they discussed it with the children during construction, after completion, and after the children had occupied their "domain" for a period of days.

From ten experiments the investigators made some tentative observations, though they warned that their findings might not be relevant for other age groups, cultures, or environments. First, they found that, although the children were given full freedom to play with the foam, they always chose to create an environment after only a very short time of playing more rough and tumble games. Second, the groups always started by making rectangles, parallelepipeds, and then, several hours or days later, rejected them sometimes with violence, replacing them with much more expressive free forms. The children explained that they preferred to live in complicated spaces with rich shapes and much character. Third, although the children designed their spaces to fit closely with the activities to be performed in them, the activities they chose did not fall into traditional categories. They designed their places not for painting, geography, or other school subjects, but for collective work, councils, individual work, small groups, dance, and intimacy. The activities were organized by the children according to the similarity of their psycho-

logical impact.

The investigators suggested that their experiments not only revealed some of the different ways children design places, they also allowed children to learn from the process; most notably, their awareness of architectural surroundings increased, extending even from this one experience to other settings. They also observed that "the details [the children] reported to us in their increasing awareness of the relations between 'inside' and 'outside' seemed to us to be a strong indication of the 'territorial' qualities children needed, to feel at ease and secure."[14] The authors are modest in their conclusions but their experiments stand out as a unique, open investigation of children's spontaneous architecture.[15]

Institutional Attempts to Encourage Children's Architecture. "Adventure playgrounds," where children are able to build their own places out of loose parts, were conceived in Denmark during World War II and developed rapidly after the war, first in Scandinavia and then throughout Western Europe.[16] Joe Benjamin, one of the English pioneers of adventure playgrounds, describes the architecture of these miniature cities as "ranging from the primitive kinds of dens that were traditional, that went back thousands of years, to much more sophisticated houses, shops, what we called community dens such as fire stations, hospitals, cap shops and so on."[17] Adventure playgrounds have failed to develop to any large extent in the U.S.A. because, it seems, of the ugliness and anarchy that parents believe they bring.[18] They are, however, a wonderful idea for children from the age of eight or nine years through their teens, particularly when they live in otherwise sterile residential environments.[19]

Many school teachers have seen the value of allowing children to build spaces and then play out dramas in them.[20] A particularly exciting recent example of this is the Los Angeles-based "City Building Education Programs" designed by Doreen Nelson. Although the physical building of a model city is only one part of a large carefully sequenced curriculum, it is a very important phase in igniting interest and in expressing spatially the complex political, and economic phenomena that make up a city.[21]

In the past few years, architects have been participating in schools in a large program called "Architects in Residence," funded by the National Endowment for the Arts. Although most of their projects emphasize the teaching of design to children rather than learning from them or with them about their design ideas, the numerous books that describe these projects are valuable for anyone thinking of doing architecture with children.[22]

Footnotes/A Focus...

1. At the Junior Arts Center we teach our visitors that art consists not merely of objects on pedestals or paintings on walls; it is a language that goes beyond obtaining appropriate skills to become a vocabulary for one's personal expression.

For further readings on visitor participation and accessibility in museums and galleries see:

Nancy Walch, "Inner Action with Art: Or Getting Beyond the Label," *The Aesthetic Eye: Teacher to Teacher Talk,* The Aesthetic Eye Project, National Endowment for the Humanities and the Office of the Los Angeles County Superintendent of Schools, November 1976.

Nancy Walch, "Making the Visual Arts Accessible: Whose Responsibility Is It?" *Roundtable Reports,* Vol. 4, No. 3, 1979.

Footnotes/Chairs, Boxes...

1. R.A. Hart, *Children's Experience of Place,* New York: Irvington, 1978.

2. M. Spivack, "Archetypal Place," *Architectural Forum,* 1978, pp.44-50.

3. Susan Isaacs, *Social Development in Young Children,* New York: Harcourt Brace, 1933.

4. Bernard Rudofsky, *Prodiguous Builder,* New York: Harcourt, Brace, Jovanovich, 1977, pp.350-365.

5. Lucy Sprague-Mitchell, *Young Geographers,* New York: Bank Street College of Education, 1934.

6. Susana Millar, *The Psychology of Play,* London: Penguin, 1968; and J.S. Bruner, A. Jolly, & K. Sylva, *Play: Its Role in Development and Evolution,* New York: Penguin, 1976.

7. Isaacs, *Social Development.*

8. Isaacs, *Social Development.*

9. M. Eliade, *The Sacred and the Profane: The Nature of Religion,* New York: Harvest Books, 1965.

10. Spivack, "Place," pp.44-50.

11. *Childhood City Newsletter,* Environmental Psychology Program, City University of New York, 33 W. 42nd St., N.Y. 10036.

12. For other studies in which children design through drawings but do not build a finished product, refer to:

Jose Muntanola-Thornberg, "The Child's Conception of Places to Live In," *Proceedings of the Environmental Design Research Association, Fourth Annual Conference,* Stroudsberg, PA: Dowden, Hutchinson & Ross, 1973.

Jose Muntanola-Thornberg, *La Arquitectura Como Lugar,* Barcelona: Gustavo Gili, 1975.

Jose Muntanola-Thornberg, *Strategies for the Invention of Architectural Objects.* Unpublished manuscript available from the author, School of Architecture, University of Barcelona, Spain, 1982.

13. Jean Boris & Hirschler Genevieve, "Living space imagined and actualized by children," *Cahier Sandoz,* No. 19, Edition Sandoz, 1971.

14. Boris & Hirschler, "Space."

15. Charles Zerner, *The Alligator Learning Experience: Children's Strategies and Approaches to a Design Problem,* UCLA: Proceedings of the Third Annual Conference of the Environmental Design Research Association, 1972.

16. A. Bengtsson, *Adventure Playgrounds,* New York: Praeger, 1972; and Jack Lambert & Jenny Pearson, *Adventure Playgrounds,* Harmondsworth, Middlesex, England: Penguin, 1974.

17. *Childhood City Newsletter,* 1980, No.23, 1981, p.21.

18. Clare Cooper, "Adventure Playgrounds," in *Landscape Architecture,* 1970, *61*(1), pp.18-29 and 88-91.

19. International Association for the Child's Right to Play. Muriel Otter, Secretary, 12 Cherry Tree Drive, Sheffield S11 9AE, England.

20. Sprague-Mitchell, *Geographers.*

21. Doreen Nelson, *The Center for City Building Education Programs: Position Paper,* Los Angeles: Center for City Building Education Programs, 1978.

22. A. Erickson, "Learning About the Built Environment," *National Elementary Principal,* *55*(4), 1980.

opposite
**Sleeping Beauty's castle,
Disneyland, California**
above, top
**Facade, La Casa Grande,
Hearst Castle,
San Simeon, California**
above, bottom
**House, Southern California,
ca 1969**
right
**Chateau d'Azay,
Le Rideau, France,
16th C**

The notion that artists belong in the category of children who only partly grew up is based on the quite reasonable presumption that those qualities we admire so much in children's drawings and constructions, their spontaneity and their vulnerability, are present in the work of a few adults who never lost those qualities; they are, as Aldous Huxley put it in Point Counterpoint, *the "eternal adolescents through whom the race matures." We have already seen, in our first group of exhibitions, how a number of today's most prominent artists have employed building materials to construct or sculpt a sense of place in their art. Other artists, less prominent perhaps and more influenced by the child's sense of wonder, have created special places too; for the most part, theirs are much more literal representations of childhood dreams and of a far grander scale than the ones to be formed in galleries.*

"The Vernacular Castle" introduces the work of adults who have hung onto some of the fantasies of children, and have transformed their houses (or a corner of their back yard, or their garage) into castles that are often full of the fairy-tale imagery of the real medieval ones. Then, at the University of Southern California, there is an exhibition on the grandest of all the California castles, William Randolph Hearst's fantasyland at San Simeon, designed by the architect Julia Morgan. Julia Morgan, the first woman to graduate from the Ecole des Beaux Arts, in Paris, is far from anonymous, or naive; neither was William Randolph Hearst. And San Simeon is not the house of a slave born on the property of his master, or indeed of everyday people at all; but the enormous presence here of fantasy and of dreams, and such innocent dreams of long ago and far away, seem to us to earn this opulent structure a proper place in an exhibition on vernacular architecture.
—P.B.

OR
CHILDREN
GROWN
UP

**Mary Ann
Beach Harrel**

THE VERNACULAR CASTLE

In man's long search for a secure dwelling place, the castle has given him his greatest sense of protection, at first with its physical walls, and later with crenellated images of them or metaphorical allusions to them. From the massive hilltop fortifications of medieval Europe to Horace Walpole's Strawberry Hill in Gothic Revival England to William Randolph Hearst's San Simeon in Spanish Colonial Revival California to the multiply locked and television-monitored condominiums of present-day America, a man's home has continued to be his castle.

The form of the castle began, undoubtedly, as a prehistoric encampment, a hill surrounded by ditches and mounds of earth, and then slowly evolved, keeping pace to one degree or another with advances that were made in the art of laying siege. The development of castles was probably the longest enduring and most seriously adhered to case in history of form following function. The first large structure was a single tower, or keep, square in plan and several stories high, usually just one big room on top of another. At some point it was discovered that round towers gave a better view of the land below, with fewer blind spots and more structural strength. Then a wall was placed around the keep to provide an extra layer of defense and a little more space, allowing the inhabitants to live somewhat less vertically. As the castle population expanded or as the enemies grew more proficient, more walls were added, often in concentric rings. These walls, which began to sprout towers of their own, grew thicker as battering rams got bigger, higher as siege towers and catapaults got stronger, and deeper as mining underneath them became more popular. Machicolations, the slight projections along the upper walls, were found to prevent enemy scalers from reach-

ing the top, as did the boiling oil that could be poured from holes in their lower edges. Moats and drawbridges protected the walls even more, while crenellations along the top and slit windows farther down became excellent places to launch a counter-offensive. With the coming of gunpowder, the walls were given sweeping curves so that cannon balls might glance off, but this scheme was not entirely successful; it was not long before an altogether different approach to defense had to be considered, namely the forming together of nations and of standing armies.

During its zenith between the tenth and fifteenth centuries, the castle was the single most important stabilizing element in an extremely volatile Western Europe. There were a great many of them: Germany had some 10,000 castles, France 20,000, Spain 2,500, and Belgium 900. That such small

populations with so few tools took it upon themselves to build so many large and intricate structures indicates how fundamental these were to the survival of their societies. After long-range artillery had made castles obsolete, many were used as quarries for new buildings, but some castles were given over to new uses, so significant were they to the towns that their huge walls still dominated. Old castles became palaces, country estates, military bases, administrative centers, and museums.

Even though its original function was gone, the castle, as an image of absolute strength, burned on in people's minds, as powerful as ever; it was carried all the way to America and across it to California. And for good reason: it was the consistent impregnability of these medieval strongholds, as much as anything else, that had allowed the early development of European and, as a result, American culture, its political and social organization, codes of honor, language, literature, and laws. As the years went by, these powerful images began to be softened by romance, especially in the hands of Sir Walter Scott and innumerable other novelists and poets. Castles were no longer seen as instruments of war as much as they were beautiful settings for deeds of chivalry and labors of love. By the latter part of the eighteenth century, architects and architectural propounders could live with these pent-up passions no more and so launched a Gothic, or medieval, revival that swept across Europe, and, more than a half a century later, made its way to America. Public buildings began to look something like cathedrals, and houses began to look like castles. For the homeowner, the Gothic Revival provided an opportunity to confirm in stone what he had continued to believe for several centuries, that once inside his own rooms, however mean and cramped, he was a king.

This notion of personal sovereignty was particularly widespread in the United States, a land well-known for its hardy individuals. But this land of such unprecedented independence and opportunity was, at the same time, almost completely devoid of any historical tradition. The American had to borrow his history and culture from his forebears in Europe including, of course, his architecture. For the European, the grandest, or at least the largest, symbol of his culture was his castle, still clinging to the hill at the center of town. But Americans did not have any castles; even their few log forts were off in the wilderness somewhere, rotting away. What they did have was a vivid image of the European castle, which was given an extra breadth of romance by the distance afforded by the expanse of the Atlantic Ocean and so burned even brighter in the American mind than in that of the European.

This mixture, then, of American preoccupation with independence and its romantic yearning for a history made the American home-owner especially prone to see his house in terms of impenetrable walls and battlements and defensible towers. Before the Industrial Revolution had produced its mass workers and mass housing, almost every person in America either built a castle or dreamed of building one, from the grand estates and plantation houses to the tiniest cottages and, particularly poignant, the lonely farmhouses and cabins on the plains; most of them did not look at all like castles, but they were regarded as such by their fond owners.

The Gothic Revival style hit this continent in the middle of the nineteenth century and, despite the sale of a great many pattern books,

opposite, left
Castle, 15th C
right
Castle, 16th C

below, left
House, Northern California, ca 1970
below, right
Garage, Berkeley, California, ca 1920

most notably by Andrew Jackson Downing, it broke apart into an endless number of variations. The first American Gothic Revival houses were modeled after the ones in England: they were big, made of stone, and looked like castles; as in England, only the rich could afford them. But this was America, a land composed of willful common men and resourceful carpenters with minds and newly invented scroll saws of their own. Using wood instead of stone because it was cheap, readily available, and more easily worked, they seized upon this opportunity to make every man's dream a more literal reality. All across the nation, the Gothic tracery and corbels and crockets and finials of Europe were sawn carefully out of white pine, Douglas fir, and redwood. And then, because this was America, they were duplicated less precisely; profusely ornamented screens and brackets and bargeboards, hardly any two alike, began to make the small houses of America look less like miniature castles or even miniature cathedrals than they did liberally iced gingerbread cakes.

The last half of the nineteenth century saw the revival in the United States of almost every architectural style known to man. Some of these managed to look more like castles even than their Gothicky antecedents: the Italianate, the Queen Anne, and the Eastlake styles, for instance, all sported prominent towers; the Richardsonian Romanesque combined enormous towers with massive stone walls. These freely adapted American fantasies, most of them based on European models, continued to be widely popular until the 1930s, when the sober geometry of a more up-to-date European import, the International Style, began to lay on its own siege.

But there has been another castle building tradition in this country,

a small but solid part of American vernacular architecture that has followed its own path to the present day, influenced hardly at all by the comings and goings of the formally accepted styles and movements. This is the realm of houses that look a great deal like castles, not just subtle illusions or metaphorical allusions, but full-blown, crenellated and turreted and drawbridged bastions. Most of them have been constructed, usually by hand, by a long line of eccentrics whose vision of what a house should be was not much different from that of most Americans, but whose literal and sometimes monomaniacal interpretations of that vision have placed them somewhere beyond the edge of even American individuality.

It is not surprising, therefore, that a disproportionate number of these vernacular castles have been made in California, which was famous even before the '49ers ar-

rived as a land of golden opportunity, realized fantasies, independent thought, and eccentrics. In general, however, Californians have not led their lives much differently from the rest of the country; they have just tended, like the castle builders, to do it in the extreme. While almost any neighborhood in America will include Cotswold cottages, Tudor mansions, Spanish missions, Italian villas, Swiss chalets, and a few Southern plantation houses, Califor-

nia has streets and streets of them, often lined up one after another, each one screaming out its acquired, one-facade-thick ethnicity. But even in California, the literal castles are a breed apart: there are not a lot of them and they are usually hard to find. Still, there is an astonishing number of variations within this narrow theme: castles come in all sizes and in almost every price range, degree of literalness, and style — there is even a

California Ranch Style castle. There are many kinds of castle makers as well, from do-it-yourself builders and remodellers to reputable architects; indeed, hard as it might seem to believe, a few developers have been known to build castles for speculation.

In choosing examples for this exhibit, we have wanted to display this range as broadly as possible while concentrating on those castles that most clearly and en-

thusiastically represented the personal visions of their owners. To that end, we have made only one general limitation: all the examples had to have been designed by people without formal training in design. That all of our examples come from California reflects to a degree our regional predilection, but it mostly reflects the strange predilection of the state itself.

opposite, left
Standon Hall, Hayward, California, ca 1919
right
House, Hollywood, California, 1977-78

above
House, near Monterey, California, 1979
left
House, Southern California, ca 1969

Carla Fantozzi

By 1919, architecture in the Spanish style was recoginzed as distinctively Californian. Both Mission and Spanish Colonial styles, usually in eclectic mix, "...bring to the mind but one thought — a group of buildings scattered over Southern California...Instantly the mind pictures a warm and sunny climate, a group of palm and magnolia trees, in the shadow of which nestles a low rambling building..."[1] In 1924, an architectural critic, Felix Rey, writing in the influential journal *Architect and Engineer of California*, summarized the state's passion, then rising to its height,for Spanish building: "Give me neither Romanesque nor Gothic; much less Italian Renaissance, and least of all English Colonial — This is California — give me Mission."[2] However, that same period, the mid-1920s, also saw a great many local architects adapting the elements of styles from around the nation and the world to California's congenial topography and semi-tropical climate. Greene and Greene's 1908 Gamble House in Pasadena reflected the simplifying, conservative nature of the Arts and Crafts Movement. In 1923, Frank Lloyd Wright transcended his Prairie Style in concrete block in the Millard House in Pasadena. With Dr. Phillip Lovell's Beach House (Newport Beach, 1925-26) and his Los Angeles home (1927), Rudolph Schindler and Richard Neutra brought the highly geometric International Style to Southern California. But in the midst of this flourishing of avant-garde and revival sytles, the advocates of the Spanish Colonial and Mission Revival styles argued, with obvious success, that their persuasions were the most suitable for the southwestern environment and, even more important, were based on historical precedent, the Hispanic settlement of California.

As the first Spanish settlers had discovered, California's Mediterranean climate and its indigenous

HEARST CASTLE

The Creation of a California Monument

building materials, adobe brick and plaster, allowed them to recall the architectural styles they were accustomed to in Southern Europe. In article after article and book after book, such turn-of-the-century architects and architectural critics as George Wharton James, Rexford Newcomb, R.S. Requa, and R.W. Sexton expounded on the simplicity and freedom from affectation of the Spanish style and argued for a selective use of Iberian motifs that was sensitive to the landscape and the environment and the indigenous building traditions. James wrote in 1903: "It must be confessed, however, that such a climate and such surroundings are needed in order to justify such an architecture...So we are content that this Mission style should be regarded as a distinctive possession of that earthly paradise of which Californians are so justly proud."[3]

Other writers at the time, con-cerned with the development of an American architectural style encouraged each locality to select an already existing persuasion, usually from Europe, that was appropriate to its own heritage; however, the adaptation of such an imported style to American life was held to be crucial.[4] R.S. Requa, the avid proponent of Spanish architecture for California, suggested that an American architecture could be found through an eclectic study of world architecture. In the foreword to *Old World Inspiration for American Architecture* (1929), he explained that measured drawings were not included in order to stimulate creativity rather than to encourage imitation. "Not until we initiate instead of imitate..., can we hope for real architecture in America, architecture that will persist unaffected by transient fads and fancies, architecture that will fulfill its purposes and justify its use."[5]

In this context Southern California

developed an indigenous vernacular architecture based on the Spanish tradition. David Gebhard has observed that in twentieth-century America, "there has been only one brief period of time and only one restricted geographic area in which there existed anything approaching a unanimity of architectural form. This was the period from approximately 1920 through the early 1930s, when the Spanish Colonial or Mediterranean Revival was virtually the accepted norm in Southern California."[6] It was during the formative period of this style in 1919, that William Randolph Hearst (1863-1951) decided to build an estate at San Simeon, California, on a mountain where he had gone camping with his father and later his own family.

The design was hardly begun before Hearst realized that he was, in fact, very much concerned with building a California monument. What had started as a simple bungalow on the crest of Camp Hill evolved into a complex recreational retreat that included a main building, La Casa Grande, and three flanking guest houses, La Casa del Mar (House A), La Casa del Monte (House B), and La Casa del Sol (House C). The first discussions about style were made with his architect Julia Morgan (1892-1957) in her San Francisco office, and by letter and cable. A letter of December 31, 1919, from Hearst to Julia Morgan suggests Hearst's direct influence in defining the Spanish character of the building program:

I have thought a great deal over whether to make this whole group of buildings Baroc [sic], in the Eighteenth Century style, or Renaissance.

It is quite a problem. I started out with the Baroc idea in mind, as nearly all the Spanish architecture in America is of that character; and

the plaster surfaces that we associate all Spanish architecture in California with are a modification of that style, as I understand it.

If we should decide on this style, I would at least want to depart from the very crude and rude examples of it that we have in our early California Spanish Architecture.

The Mission at Santa Barbara is doubtless the highest example of this California architecture, and yet it is very bare and almost clumsy to my mind.

The best things that I have seen in this Spanish Baroc are at the San Diego Exposition... I would advise sending photographers and architectural draughtsmen down to the San Diego Exposition to get pictures and drawings of exteriors and interiors and of de-

tails, so as to have a lot of stuff at our disposal and for our guidance...

The alternative is to build this group of buildings in the Renaissance style of Southern Spain. We picked out the towers of the Church of Ronda. I suppose they are Renaissance or else transitional, and they have some Gothic feeling; but a Renaissance decoration, particularly that of the very southern part of Spain, would harmonize well with them...

The trouble would be, I suppose, that it has no historic association with California, or rather with the Spanish architecture in California.

I would very much like to have your views on what we should do in regard to this group of buildings, what style of architecture we should

select. I think the Renaissance decoration can be adapted to the smooth plaster surfaces. I think it is so in the Church of Ronda and in certain cities in the South of Spain and in the Balaeric Islands. They call it Pateresque [sic]...

Julia Morgan's letter of January 8, 1920 suggests by its diplomacy her respect for the active role Hearst assumed in designing the castle:

Two years ago work took

below, left
Panama-California Exposition, San Diego, California, 1915
below, center
Mission, Santa Barbara, California
below, right
Church of Santa Maria La Mayor, Ronda, Spain

below, left
La Casa Grande, *front elevation, Julia Morgan*
below, right
Facade of La Casa Grande

prevailing Beaux-Arts tradition enabled this avid, though amateur, patron and cultivated architect to construct a monument that was specifically Californian in character and evocative of high Spanish art, and was a flamboyant social statement as well. Although present-day critics tend to denigrate Hearst's aristocratic and autocratic motive,[9] the relation between social status and architectural form was already nationally recognized practice. Hearst's decision to use original Spanish style rather than the California architecture that had come from it marked, in fact, a refinement in the eclectic approach. In contrast to the random juxtaposition of transplanted styles in Newport, Rhode Island, Hearst's Spanish castle reflected a conspicuous sense of appropriateness. By taking an expansive view of Spanish architecture, Hearst and Morgan were able to refine the provincial qualities of the Mission style and

combine a variety of more elaborate Spanish styles while remaining consistent with the developing character of California architecture. The buildings of the San Diego Panama California International Exposition of 1915 conveniently mark the beginning of this employment of different types of Iberian architecture to suit a variety of tastes.[10] So, by 1915 definitions, Hearst's castle is just as much a part of California's tradition as any of the 21 Spanish missions.

Julia Morgan was an eclectic architect, trained at the Ecole des Beaux-Arts in Paris, and, as a result, was adaptable and versatile in a variety of styles that could appeal to Hearst. But the San Simeon project demanded much more than just a knowledge of styles; the job was both extremely challenging and tedious, and it often required a great deal of patience. Biographers have noted the special relationship that existed between

me down to San Diego very frequently and I know the buildings well. The composition and decoration are certainly very well handled indeed, but I question whether this type of decoration would not seem too heavy and clumsy on our buildings, because while the Exposition covers acres with its buildings, we have a comparatively small group, and it would seem to me that they should charm by their detail rather than overwhelm by more or less clumsy exuberance.

I feel just as you do about the early California Mission Style as being too primitive to be gone back to and copied. Charming as they are in mass and color, I believe their appeal is because of their simple, direct expression of their object. As I wrote you in

my last letter, I believe we could get something really very beautiful by using the combination of Ronda Towers and the Sevilla doorway, with your Virgin over it and San Simeo and San Christophe on either side. This would allow for great delicacy and at the same time, brilliance in the decoration, and I see how it could be executed without running into a very great expense.[8]

This typical exchange of proposal and qualification indicates that, besides his interest in creating a California monument, Hearst wished to associate his castle with the more elaborate kinds of Spanish architecture, even Churrigueresque; Morgan, though, was interested in a more delicate combination of Spanish sophistication and Mission simplicity. The atmosphere of eclecticism encouraged by the

two reveals how their enterprise evolved as well as how Hearst directed her activities. In a letter of December 27, 1919, he writes,

I suppose you have the books and pictures I sent by this time. I am trying to find things that will make these little houses interesting and distinct even, not at all like the ordinary bungalows...

I hope you will see your way to work in those carved and colored cornices in the Moorish style, and to use some tiling for the frieze and perhaps in other places where it will be effective. I think this will take the cottages away from the bungalow look, and give them a character which is perfectly appropriate as many of the buildings of Southern Spain have this motif in their architecture.[12]

gram on March 17, 1920 to Julia Morgan: "All the little houses are stunning and the slightly different treatment makes them very attractive. I think you are right about House B. Please complete them before I can think up any more changes."[13] Nevertheless, on the very next day, he suggested modifications: "Would it not be better to lengthen the view bedrooms of House B even if we had to use the same treatment as that of House C."[14] Walter Steilberg, an employee of Julia Morgan, who designed much of the structural concrete work at San Simeon, recalled that Hearst once had a fireplace moved from one side of a room to another and then back again because it looked better before.[15]

Structural changes were not as challenging for Julia Morgan as was Hearst's desire to incorporate into the buildings the multitude of historical artifacts he was busy collecting, often in wholesale lots, from

patron and architect. In *Citizen Hearst*, W.A. Swanberg observes that with the exceptions of Miss Marion Davies and his wife, Julia Morgan was the most important woman in Hearst's life.[11]

Hearst was a willful man of strong personal tastes who was determined to have his vision realized in stone on top of Camp Hill. Julia Morgan willingly made herself an instrument for the implementation of his plans. It was Hearst himself,

using books and pictures he had acquired in his travels or from dealers, who directed Julia Morgan's attention to examples that he wanted to incorporate into his buildings. When Julia Morgan was at San Simeon, Hearst would give her his undivided attention, listening to her suggestions about style. Her primary duty, however, was to engineer the construction of this enormous dream.

Correspondence between the

Normally, Morgan would respond immediately with a series of drawings, which Hearst would return with comments scrawled all over them. He also communicated with numerous cables.

During construction, Hearst would often change his mind and suggest alterations. On occasion he would acknowledge his chronic indecisiveness but also took humorous pride in the copiousness of his ideas. For example, he sent a tele-

above, left, top
Upper decorative band, window grille, Assembly Room, La Casa Grande
Julia Morgan
above, left, bottom
Roof cornice detail, La Casa Grande
above, center
Facade of La Casa del Sol
above, right
La Casa del Sol, study,
Julia Morgan

around the world. Ironwork, tile, architectural sculpture and fragments, cabinet work, ceilings, paneling, and choir stalls were continually being shipped from Europe to the Hill for installation. In a letter of May 23, 1920, we see something of Hearst's pragmatic method for purchasing works of art:

I have bought some more stuff at the last auction sale of the season. I am sending it in a third car, which should arrive in about a month from date.

It contains a pair of very excellent doors, carved on both sides, which can be used for the main entrance door of Cottage A.

I am also sending a couple of window grills, matched, which can go over the windows on either side of the door of this house...[16]

This reservoir of materials was at Julia Morgan's disposal; what had not been procured already, Hearst's agents would seek out in Spain or elsewhere. A letter of December 30, 1919 suggests the variety and great quantity of material that Hearst was so enthusiastically making available:

I am enclosing also a Stanford White room (photograph) from the residence of Payne Whitney. I think I have one door frame similar to the one shown in this room, and I am hoping to buy another one somewhat similar, which came out of Mrs. Lydig's house, which Stanford White also did.

The ceilings I cannot get, so we will have to copy some of these that we get glimpses of in these pictures.

I can buy three large important window grills and also a tremendous big door grill... Can we use them? They are genuine...[17]

Craftsmen were employed to extend and join Hearst's treasures; and under Morgan's direction they duplicated such ceilings and all other types of decorative embellishments, whether in wood, iron, tile, or plaster. Hearst often preferred local craftsmen: "I do not believe...in relation to the two fountains that they would be any cheaper made in Rome than they would be made in California...I suggest, therefore, that you go ahead and have these fountains made in California and that we begin on them immediately so that they may be ready and erected as soon as possible."[18] Working from photographs and books that included measured drawings for the details, the local craftsmen managed to modify the ancient parts to fit the new structure. Just as the Greek innkeeper, Procrustes, had chopped off or stretched his guests to fit his iron bed, Hearst's employees were able to accommodate most of his requests: "What will be dimensions of rooms in Towers of C. Have wonderful genuine ceiling for one which could be duplicated on other."[19]

Arthur and Mildred Byne, former curators of Architecture and Allied Arts at the Hispanic Society in New York, supplied Hearst with many of his Spanish artifacts, books on Spanish art and architecture, and measured drawings and photographs of architectural fragments.[20] Under the auspices of the Hispanic Society they had published scholarly books and illustrated manuals on a variety of topics relating to Spanish art and architecture.[21] Writing to Julia Morgan on October 1, 1921, Mildred Stapley-Byne explained how they came to be dealers of Spanish art:

Knowing, as we now do, the charm of the traditional Spanish house we envy you architects of California your opportunity to create something fine in this line. We have promised to publish a series of Andalusian cortijos, or granges, for your benefit, Andalusian being that part of Spain that most resembles California; but the Spanish Romanesque, and Spanish Furniture, both under way, put the country house far off into the future. Meanwhile, if we can't build Spanish residences, we can furnish them. Our opportunities for disposing of good old private collections were so numerous that it seemed a pity not to take advantage of them, so we have become antiquarios. My husband went...to New York and made arrangements with several decorators there to send them complete Spanish interiors or separate pieces...We were almost overwhelmed with orders and have sent off a dozen large shipments since his return...Many things are brought to our attention to be quietly sold that would never reach the ordinary dealer.[22]

With the approval of Hearst, Julia Morgan sought the Bynes's assistance, providing them with a description of the San Simeon project:

We are building for him a sort of village on a mountaintop overlooking the sea and ranges of mountains, miles from any railway, and housing, incidentally, his collections as well as his family. Having different buildings allows the use of very varied treatments.[23]

So far we have received from him, to incorporate in the new buildings, some 12 or 13 carloads of antiques, brought from the ends of the earth and from prehistoric down to late Empire in period, the majority, however, being of Spanish origin...I don't see myself where we are ever going to use half suitably, but I find that the idea is to try things out and if they are not satisfactory, discard them for the next that comes that promises better. There is interest and charm coming gradually into play.[24]

Soon, the Bynes became one of Hearst's major suppliers of Spanish furnishings and building parts. On November 16, 1921, Hearst wrote to Morgan:

I note that the letter from Mildred Stapley-Byne says that [the cornice from] the Casa Valle Santorio has also been sold..

In as much as this lady says that she and her husband have gone into the antique business, maybe she could trace this cornice and if found try to buy it for us. Also, please correspond with the lady and ask her to act as agent for us. We will want a tremendous lot of stuff for the big house, bath house, etc. and probably we could do much better from her than from the average antiquary.[25]

Hearst was so pleased with the Bynes that he gave them a continuing subsidy to purchase items on his behalf, though in later years it became increasing difficult to export works of art from Spain.[26]

Construction on San Simeon continued well into the 1930s, although there was a temporary halt in 1936 due to hard times in the Hearst empire. Still, Hearst and Julia Morgan continued to plan new wings and new buildings, with Hearst studying and modifying the drawings as meticulously as he had the earlier designs. A few of the schemes were built, but they were constrained by a limited budget and lacked the former opulence.

Bearing the marks of Hearst's scrutiny, the drawings for Hearst Castle from the collection of California Polytechnic State University, San Luis Obispo, provide a rare opportunity to study the creative collaboration between architect and patron, between amateur and professional. We see how fundamentally important Hearst was in determining the physical character of his house and how, through his choice of an Hispanic architectural style, he was able to adapt old world forms to create a monument in what had become the California vernacular style.

Footnotes

1. George C. Baum, ''The Mission Type,'' in Henry H. Saylor, *Architectural Styles for Country Houses*, New York: Robert M. McBride & Co., 1919, p.67.

2. Felix Rey, ''A Tribute to Mission Style,'' *Architect and Engineer*, vol. LXXIX, October 1924, p.78.

3. George Wharton James, ''The Influence of the Mission Style Upon the Civic and Domestic Architecture of Modern California,'' *Draftsman*, vol. 5, no. 5, 1903, p.469.

4. R.W. Sexton, *Spanish Influence on American Architecture and Decoration*, New York: Brentanos, 1927, p.9.

5. R.S. Requa, *Old World Inspiration for American Architecture*, Los Angeles: Monolith Portland Cement Co., 1929, Foreword, *i*.

6. David Gebhard, *George Washington Smith, 1876-1930*, Santa Barbara: The Art Gallery University of California, 1964, Introduction.

7. Hearst to Morgan, December 31, 1919. All letters to or from Morgan quoted in this essay are from the Julia Morgan Correspondence, California Polytechnic University, San Luis Obispo.

8. Morgan to Hearst, January 8, 1920.

9. See also: Walter Kidney, ''Another Look at Eclecticism,'' *Progressive Architecture*, vol. 48, no. 9, September 1967, pp.118-127, and Paul Goldberger, ''Towards a New International Style,'' *New York Times Interior Design Magazine*, September 27, 1982.

10. David Gebhard, ''The Spanish Colonial Revival in Southern California (1895-1930),'' *Journal of the Society of Architectural Historians*, vol. 26, May 1967, p.136.

11. W.A. Swanberg, *Citizen Hearst*, New York: Charles Scribner's Sons, 1961, p.491.

12. Hearst to Morgan, December 27, 1919.

13. Hearst to Morgan, March 17, 1920.

14. Hearst to Morgan, March 18, 1920.

15. Walter Steilberg, *Address delivered before the Historical Guide Association of California*, Unpublished, Bancroft Library, University of California, Berkeley, August 1966, p.8.

16. Hearst to Morgan, May 23, 1920.

17. Hearst to Morgan, December 30, 1919.

18. Hearst to Morgan, January 5, 1922.

19. Hearst to Morgan, February 24, 1922.

20. Hispanic Society, *A History of the Hispanic Society of America*, New York: Hispanic Society, 1945, p.544.

21. Some of their more well-known works:

Arthur and Mildred Byne, *Forgotten Shrines of Spain*, Philadelphia: Lippincott & Co., 1926.
—*Provincial Houses in Spain*, New York: William Helbern, Inc., 1925.
—*Rejeria of the Spanish Renaissance*, New York: Hispanic Society Publications, 1914.
—*Spanish Architecture of the Sixteenth Century*, New York: G. Putnam's, 1917.
—*Spanish Interiors and Furniture*, 3 vols., New York: William Welburn, Inc., 1921.

22. Mildred Stapley-Byne to Morgan, October 1, 1921.

23. Morgan to Byne, September 19, 1921.

24. Morgan to Byne, November 18, 1921.

25. Hearst to Morgan, November 16, 1921.

26. As early as 1925 the Bynes had trouble exporting works of art:

''. . .I have just returned from a tour of Spain in quest of a suitable palace for Hearst. I had a half-dozen in mind before starting out as being likely prizes but some had to be abandoned because of difficulty of securing permission for exportation. Where a building has been declared a National Monument there is no hope at all; where it has been declared a Provincial Monument there is hope but untold red-tape and difficulties. So we are more or less limited to little-known and abandoned edifices well off the beaten track. Fortunately, years of wandering over the country in connection with our books has put me in touch with almost everything of interest. . .''

Byne to Morgan, November 5, 1925.

Bibliography

Aidala, Thomas. *Hearst Castle: San Simeon*. New York: Hudson Hills Press, 1981.

Gebhard, David. ''Spanish Colonial Revival in Southern California (1895-1930),'' *Journal of the Society of Architectural Historians*, Vol. 26, May 1967: pp.131-147.

Hamlin, T.F. ''California Whys and Wherefores,'' *Pencil Points*, Vol. XXII, May 1914: pp.339-344.

Jacobs, Stephen W. ''California Contemporaries of Frank Lloyd Wright, 1885-1915,'' in *Problems of the 19th and 20th Centuries*, Vol. IV. Princeton: Princeton University Press, 1963, p.34-63.

James, George Wharton. ''The Influence of the Mission Style upon the Civic and Domestic Architecture of Modern California,'' *Craftsman*, Vol. 5, no. 5, 1903: pp.458-469, 567.

Kirker, Harold. *California's Architectural Frontier*. Santa Barbara: Peregrine Smith Inc., 1973.

Newcomb, Rexford. *The Spanish House for America*. Philadelphia: J.B. Lippincott Co., 1927.

Requa, R.S. *Old World Inspiration for American Architecture*. Los Angeles: Monolith Portland Cement Co., 1929.

Roth, Leland M. *A Concise History of American Architecture*. New York: Harper and Row Publishers, 1979.

Sexton, R.W. *Spanish Influence on American Architecture and Decoration*. New York: Brentanos, 1927.

Whiffen, Marcus. *American Architecture Since 1780*. Cambridge, Mass.: MIT Press, 1981.

opposite
**Adobe ruin, Truchas,
New Mexico**
above, top
**An Old Adobe, woodblock,
Frank C, Barks, 1939**
above, center
**Casa Estudillo,
San Diego, California, 1820**
above, bottom
**Rancho Santa Rosa,
Santa Barbara County,
California, ca 1840**

One of the characteristics of vernacular buildings, or of functional commonplace buildings made anywhere, or of special buildings, even, made by people of limited resources is that they are made out of some straightforward something, out of some material or set of materials, generally indigenous to the place, which help to relate a building to its site; generally, in times before our own, these materials were most inexpensively and conveniently obtained somewhere nearby, in some way therefore almost always altogether appropriate.

In the American Southwest, in the territory through which people came overland to Los Angeles, one of the most prevalent materials was adobe. And in Mexico, too, through which the Spanish settlers had earlier come, adobe blocks were the favored building material. The California Indian predilection for building temporary dwellings of brush, which could periodically be burned down along with all the varmints who had been attracted to them, went altogether unappreciated by the Indians' new Spanish lords, who sought the permanence that came with adobe, as well as the extended possibility of keeping idle hands at work. The leitmotif in the Arcadian California of everyone's dreams is the adobe ranch house, with some wood. Esther McCoy and Evelyn Hitchcock exhibit its history.
—P.B.

OF
ADOBE

**Esther McCoy
and Evelyn Hitchcock**

THE RANCH HOUSE

above
*Pio Pico Mansion,
Pico Rivera, California,
before 1891*

The California ranch house as a type existed in its early utilitarian form little longer that half a century. It originated in the 1820s to shelter a community made up of family and relations, visitors, servants, vaqueros, and herdsmen living on a vast land grant remote from populated centers. The need for the ranch house faded after the 1870s when two disastrous droughts decimated the cattle, impoverished the owners, and led to the breakup of large land holdings into smaller ranches.

The ranch house strayed as far from its roots as the word vernacular did from the original Latin *vernaculus* — "born in one's house." Like other forms of vernacular architecture, the ranch house has adjusted to new uses, new tools and materials, new roof lines, and new shapes; it has ridden out changes in the economy and changes of government and seems to thrive on everything but over-sentimentality.

The ranch house gained favor because of the sensuous appeal of its forms and materials, the reassuring massiveness of the earth walls, evident in the deep reveals of doors and windows, and the constant play of light and shadow on lightly-plastered, rude adobe brick. Then there was the strong sense of place evoked by the central patio, one of its four sides open to a distant view, the other three shaded by *corredores* which formed an easy transition between indoors and out.

The houses were built without nails, and the tools were the two hands. Builders dug and shaped the adobe and laid the bricks with a mud mortar, plastered the surface with a wash of mud or ground sea shells that were burned in the patio kiln to make lime; they roofed the walls with bundles of tule from the marshes, laid them on the precious wood of the beams, covered the tule with the brea from the tar pits, carried by cart from what is

now the grounds of the County Museum of Art, and sealed the tar with a top coat of earth.

Some of the charm of the houses was a consequence of the vulnerability of the adobe to erosion — windows and doors on almost the same plane as the exterior walls, the heavy shutters to cover the glassless window openings. The deep reveals inside were cut at a 45-degree angle, which widened them into seats in the sparsely furnished rooms and also reflected the light.

The floors were the earth, watered and tamped to a smooth finish, hard as tile. After the secularization of the missions in 1833, floor and roof tiles were appropriated from the abandoned missions. But after the Mormons established a mill in San Bernadino in 1852 and drove wagonloads of timber down to Los Angeles, the planked floor was preferred to tile.

Cavernous fireplaces with roaring fires to warm the rooms were a romantic fiction, for there was no wood to burn. If there was a fireplace it was in the kitchen and was used for roasting meat. However, the adobe absorbed the heat from the sun and from braziers, so interiors were warm in winter and cool in summer; the low winter sun struck the *corredores*, which served as daytime rooms, while the interiors were for sleeping and for storage. The extended rafters of the flat roofs supported the roofs of the *corredores*, which tempered the high summer sun.

Most ranch houses of the Spanish and Mexican periods in California were in the south where there was the greatest amount of grazing land. The primitive forerunner of the ranch house was a one-room hut of adobe brick, situated on ground high enough to protect the pebble foundation of the adobe from erosion; it was built near a spring or creek to provide water in a region of low rainfall. Roof rafters were willow poles which supported thatch or matted tule, waterproofed with mud or brea. Heat came from a brazier of coals set on the earthen floor; cooking was over a fire in the open. Around the house were no trees; even brush was cleared to prevent surprise attacks. The one low door was stretched rawhide on rawhide hinges.

The Pueblo of Los Angeles was

Los Angeles had been established as an agricultural colony rather that a presidio; the semi-arid climate produced little building material except for cottonwood, willow, small scrub pine, and, from the foothills, the large live oak, which deteriorated quickly. So there were fewer skilled builders than in the presidios to the north. Most of the building in Los Angeles was done by semi-skilled Indian labor. The pueblo remained a pas-

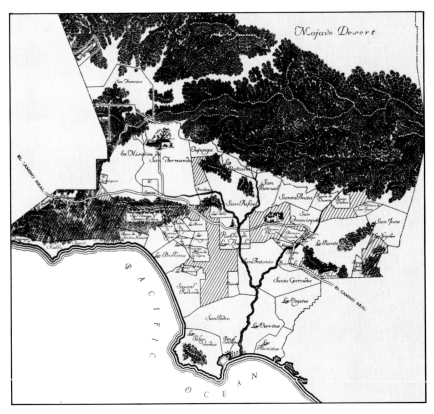

the rough cousin of the military presidios to the north and south — San Diego, Santa Barbara, Monterey, and San Francisco. Consider, for instance, that a hundred miles to the north the Santa Barbara mission was modeled on an illustration in a volume of Vitruvius that a monk had brought from Spain. Goods were shipped from Mexico only to the presidios; shipping between presidios brought wood from north to south, but nothing to Los Angeles.

toral society long after San Francisco was a port of call on the China trade route.

The Pueblo of Los Angeles, several miles inland from the coast, developed in a way unique to Alta California. The center was small, and at the edges were thousands of acres of grazing land in ranch or pueblo common land. The pattern of development was close to that of New England where the wilderness was conquered by the estab-

lishment of inland colonies. The presidios looked to the sea, and by the middle of the nineteenth century this line of communication was evident in the wood detailing (derived from the Northern European wood tradition which had influenced New England) in the Monterey houses. The plan and elevations were symmetrical, usually two rooms on each side of a central hall; windows were double hung and glazed, doors were paneled.

Change was slow in Los Angeles, but an impetus for change came after 1834 when some of the small band of people who migrated from Mexico City settled in the pueblo, where only 1500 people lived. The newcomers, with their gentler manners and fine footwear, implanted the idea of Mexican houses laid out around lushly planted courtyards with a fountain at the center, the planting visible from the house through grilled windows. Among their household goods were im-

ported mirrors and inlaid tables. Their cooking was in *hornillos* (ovens) rather than over open fires, and they were accustomed to being served at a dining table rather than from a communal pot of spiced beef and cabbage.

Near the San Francisco Embarcadero there was, by 1841, an adobe house with a dining room, and in the senora's bedroom two high-backed chairs, a New England four-poster bed, trunks for storing clothes, a white and gold French porcelain ewer and basin, and on the walls were six color prints of saints.

The golden age of the ranch house was the 1840s, after land grants had been widely distributed. Twenty-some land grants had been given before the Mexican Revolution in 1822; these were only grazing rights on Indian land, but during the Mexican period, when church land was secularized, hundreds of grants were given with few restrictions except that a house be built within a year and the owner live there part of each year.

The ranch house was modeled on the townhouse, usually laid out in a string of rooms, one opening into the next, and each room with a door to a *corredor*. The early ranch house plan often borrowed from the Mission plan in which rooms surrounded a hollow square; a wide, high *portole* led through the building for carriages to enter the courtyard. The ranch houses loosely followed the principles of the self-sufficient mission, in which workshops, granary, and mill for grinding grain were under the main roofs or in adjacent buildings. Nearby was the pit where Indians dug the adobe, mixed it with straw, and formed it into bricks to cure in the sun.

Ranch houses often started with a one-story rectangular plan, then became an L with the addition of a wing, and a U with a second wing. Second-story additions came after wood became more plentiful. By the mid-1840s there were four two-story houses in Los Angeles County (which was then double its present size) — the Hugo Reid, Bell, and Sanchez adobes, and Rancho Los Cerritos. A second story depended upon transporting large roof beams great distances, or finding strong, straight framing material for staircases and doors.

A ranch house with modest beginnings was built on a 120-mile grant of land, Rancho San Pedro, the first grant to be made during the Spanish period, the Juan Jose Dominguez grant of 1784. The six-room ranch house was built around 1826 by the grantee's grand-nephew Manuel Dominguez. Three-foot thick adobe walls were then considered optimum for supporting the material itself and the heavy roof. (The average brick was 18″ x 20″ x 6″ and weighed over 20 pounds.) Later houses, however, had walls two feet or less in thickness.

The Dominguez house, enlarged many times, finally in the Mission Revival style, lost all resemblance to the original as it swelled to a size suitable to the Claretian seminary which it became. However, the original six rooms were restored in 1976 as a history museum.

Some townhouses of the 1820s were more imposing than the original Dominguez house. One was the 12-room Estudillo house built along one entire side of the San Diego Plaza on a site that had been granted in 1827 to Jose Antonio Estudillo, a captain in the presidial company of San Diego. Completed first[1] was an L containing the family chapel, a *sala*, four bedrooms, and a dining room, which formed the west and south sides; the north wing, added soon after, enclosed third side of a patio. The family chapel was a place of worship for

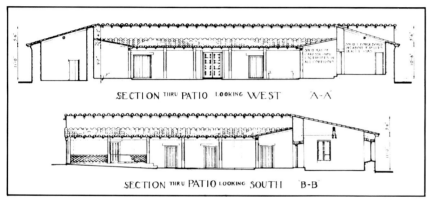

SECTION THRU PATIO LOOKING WEST   A-A

SECTION THRU PATIO LOOKING SOUTH   B-B

PIO PICO BRAND   ESTUDILLO BRAND

above, top
Elevations,
Casa Estudillo,
San Diego, California, 1820
above
Cattle Brands, San Diego
County Ranchos
right
Casa Estudillo, San Diego,
California, 1820
opposite, top
Ranch House at Santa Margarita,
Frank C. Barks, 1939
bottom, left
Plan, Casa Estudillo,
San Diego, California, 1820
bottom, right
Rancho Santa Margarita, *watercolor,*
Eva Scott Fenyes, 1913

the townspeople after the San Diego Mission was closed. Later, one of the rooms on the west side was enlarged to become a school room.

The house, restored in 1910[2], was known as "Ramona's Marriage Place," after the protagonist in the *roman a clef, Ramona.* During restoration it was determined that the shed roof had been made of logs lashed together with leather thongs. The typical bedroom in-

20-room Rancho Santa Margarita was continued on a grand scale for many years by Juan Forster. A visitor called it a "principality."

In the plan around a court was a family chapel, a wing of bunkhouses for the vaqueros, quarters for the great number of servants, and the usual social and sleeping rooms for the family and guests. Living was along the *corredores* facing the patio, the only furniture being long benches. Chickens

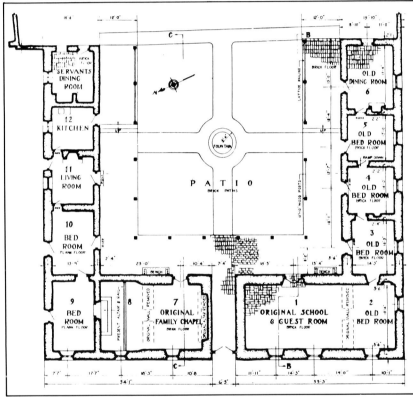

terior was 14' x 16', enclosed by three-foot adobe walls. The ceilings were somewhat higher than the average eight feet, because of the slope of the shed roof. Essentially, the townhouse in the south was as spartan as the ranch houses of the same decade.

The model of elegance of the 1830s was the two-story, 2000-square foot Larkin house in Monterey, completed in 1837 by the American Consul on a site that had

been granted him in 1835. The almost square plan, wrapped around four sides by a two-level porch, was unusual, as were the paneled doors and double-hung multi-paned windows in the numerous openings of the exterior walls.[3] A visual sense of symmetry was established in the centrally-located roof ridge, with hipped corners, and the illusion persisted despite the unequal spacing of the windows and the shaped 4" x 4" porchposts.

The floor levels were constant although the foundation followed the change in grade of the site. All interiors had molded baseboards, chair rails, and picture rails; the throat and mantelpiece of the two fireplaces had wood trim; and the newel and balustrade of the stair were turned.

Among the houses begun in the 1840s was the Rancho Santa Margarita, now the site of Camp Pendleton in San Diego County. It was located on a 125,000-acre grant of land made to Governor Pio Pico in 1841; adjoining the grant was the site of Rancho Las Flores (1844). The land was owned jointly by brothers Pio and Andres Pico until Pio bought out his brother. He presented Rancho Santa Margarita to his sister upon her marriage to Juan Forster, who was said to have paid off Pio Pico's many debts; Rancho Las Flores was a wedding gift to his son. Development of the rancho and the building of the splendid

scratched and dogs slept in the planted patio while women prepared food or sewed, and the old drowsed after the heavy mid-day meal.

The "restoration" of the hacienda for use as the commanding general's headquarters at Camp Pendleton is a romantic overlay which dims the original and largely functional character of the building. The flat roof is now low pitched and tiled, all the floors are tiled, and "furniture of the period" installed. There was an effort at authenticity in such details as the preservation of century-old planting, then an incongruous addition of an arcaded walk. The arch was exclusively a feature of the Mission style but never appeared in the early adobe residences, according to the historian Marion Parks.[4]

The popularity of Helen Hunt Jackson's 1884 novel *Ramona,* with its descriptions of hacienda life at the end of the high Mexican period as it bent to the commercialism of the American period, did much to popularize an idealized version of the ranch house.

The ranch house of the 1850s reflected growing wealth and declining simplicity. A fairly good example is the Bandini-Couts house, Guajome, near Vista. After Ysidora Bandini married Cave Johnson Couts in 1851, he sketched a floor plan for their adobe house, the 15 rooms along three sides of an unusually large patio, 80′ x 90′. A wall at one end separated the patio from the corral and stables. Ten of the rooms were used exclusively by the family, but at the end of one wing were storeroom, kitchen, and a dining room "for the Indians." At the end of the opposite wing was a blacksmith shop, and at one corner of the front facade was a room called "general merchandise." The practice of having a general store in the ranch house had begun with the American occupation, which also brought a steady flow of merchandise into the south.

Detached from the main structure of Guajome were a family chapel, barns, and sheds. A later plan of the house showed that the outbuildings had increased in number, and that the blacksmith shop was moved to one side of the corral, which was renamed "carriage court"; the former blacksmith shop became a bedroom, and the general store a study.

Guajome was pronounced a "paradise" by Judge Benjamin Hayes, who was put up at the ranch house while riding his circuit on horseback to convene court. The house took on an inappropriate picturesqueness with the addition of a tower over the entrance hall, and the heavy gates of the *portole* gave a fortresslike appearance no early ranch house ever had.

The essential features that endeared the ranch house to later generations were still there. Ranch houses were handsomely sited in a gently rolling landscape, the long low lines bespeaking the generous use of ground in the sprawling floor plan, the wings stretching out but enclosing, the private and public spaces harmoniously defined. The houses continued to turn an almost blank side to the public view, while creating intimate spaces in courts. Certainly the one-story house with all rooms in contact with the ground was more at ease in the southern landscape than the more urban two-story house, and long after wood was plentiful one-story houses were preferred in the south.

The ranch house style insinuated itself into the twentieth century single family dwellings in cities and suburbs in Southern California, subsequently spreading to other parts of the United States. Like its model, the plan sprawled, and the key to the circulation was the patio. Walls were of stucco or board-and-batten, both related to the adobe by their receptivity to light and shadow. Roofs were covered with tile, shakes, or shingles. There were often deep reveals, usually faked by widening the space between exterior and interior walls. The ranch house style was liberally mixed with Spanish Moorish, with its greater use of ornament and color.

The designations Mission, Ranch House, and Spanish Colonial styles were used interchangeably although they were distinct. The Spanish Colonial, however, relied heavily on official architecture. All of them served to keep alive in California the Mexican-Spanish experience. The only successful attempt to go beyond the surface and grapple with structure was that of Irving Gill in the first decade of the century. Gill, coming to San Diego from the Chicago office of Adler and Sullivan, was interested in experimenting with technology, and his mature style combined the revival of the flat roofs of the early houses, the sheer walls of the Mis-

sions, and the arcaded walks with the development of a structural vocabulary for the new material, reinforced concrete. Out of these elements he created a non-tangential style, which was later recognized as a forerunner of the modernist movement. Gill showed little interest in the ranch house or Spanish Colonial styles.

In the second decade of the century Bertram Goodhue brought to San Diego an authentic style from Spain (by way of Mexico): the Churrigueresque, characterized by heavy carved ornament around doors.[5] Another revival, mainly in the 1920s, was of the Monterey house by John Byers, a Santa Monica architect of unusual subtlety.

The first designer to revive the ranch house was Cliff May of San Diego. He had no training in architecture, but an intimate knowledge of early townhouses and ranch houses came from his maternal grandparents, who belonged to the Estudillo and Pedrorena families. He grew up in the first wood-framed house in San Diego, but holidays were spent with his many cousins in adobe houses. One of these was Rancho Santa Margarita, and the adjoining Rancho Las Flores, where he usually spent summer vacations.

Cliff May's first house in 1932 was built for speculation as a place to display the Mission-Mexican furniture he was designing and building. The L-shaped plan was adapted to a typical city lot. The deep-set door opened onto a *corredor* and a patio, and major rooms had direct access to these outdoor spaces. The details were more akin to the Spanish Colonial style — tile floors and roof, grilled windows, carved doors, and the arch form. He achieved the semblance of authenticity in this and his subsequent San Diego houses by mixing the buff to dark red ceramic roof and floor tiles as they came from the kiln; in this, and in the use of wrought iron hardware and lighting fixtures, he created an ambience more Spanish that Mexican.

May was far more authentic in his work of the late 1930s and '40s in Los Angeles, where both the sites and the houses were larger and the neighborhoods of low density. This allowed a greater sprawl to the plan, a major feature of the ranch house. In Los Angeles he used fewer Spanish Colonial details, relying on the U-shaped plan and the outbuildings (paddock, stables, and gatehouse) to suggest the past. Roofs were usually shingles or shakes; walls were often board-and-batten. In some of his early Los Angeles houses was a *portole* to the paddock. All rooms invariably opened to the sheltered patio, which was nearly always a splayed U.

In a 1940 Los Angeles house he flipped the plan to make a double splayed U, and by 1970 he en-

priateness to the ranch houses of the 1840s.

However, two changes did take place in his style. One was the introduction of more light through roof openings during the 1950s, when the taste of the public for lighter interiors increased. In one of his later houses he opened the roof by placing translucent strips on both sides of the ridge beam.

The other change followed the growing acceptance by the public of the open plan. This was in sharp contradiction to the walled rooms of the original ranch house, with interior partitions of thick adobe. To achieve the open plan May began to work in a post-and-beam system of construction in which the only bearing walls were exterior ones. This made it possible to use half walls and screen walls to define interior spaces. In some of his houses the ridge beam and the continuous ceiling are visible from most parts of the interior.

ease to the design that set it apart. May had caught some of the innocence and sincerity of the original, which carried the ranch house tradition into the present.

Footnotes

1. See original plan in *Historic American Buildings: California*, New York: Garland Publishing, 1980, vol. 1, p.47.

2. In 1968 it was acquired by the State Park system and restored more in sympathy with the original.

3. The double gallery came from Santo Domingo in the West Indies to the southern United States in the 1750s and from there spread throughout the South. Larkin lived in North Carolina for ten years before coming to California.

4. Marion Parks, "In Pursuit of Vanished Days: Visits to the Extant Adobe Houses of Los Angeles County, Part I," Historical Society of Southern California *Annual*, vol. XIV, no. 1, 1928, p.14.

5. Goodhue had accompanied Sylvester Baxter when he gathered material around 1900 for what was the first book in English on Spanish Colonial architecture in Mexico. Goodhue's drawings from the trip were also published.

Bibliography

Bancroft, Hubert Howe. *The Works of Hubert Howe Bancroft*. Vol. 34: *California Pastoral, 1769-1848*. San Francisco: The History Company, Publishers, 1888.

Cowan, Robert G. *Ranchos of California*. Fresno: Academy Library Guild, 1956.

Giffen, Helen S. *Casas & Courtyards: Historic Adobe Houses of California*. Foreword by W.W. Robinson. California Relations Series, no. 40. Oakland: Biobooks, 1955.

Grenier, Judson; Mason, William; et al. *A Guide to Historic Places in Los Angeles County*. Dubuque, Iowa: Kendall/Hunt Publishing Company, 1978.

Hayes, Benjamin. *Pioneer Notes from the Diaries of Judge Benjamin Hayes*

1849-1875. Los Angeles: Privately Printed, 1929.

Historic American Buildings Survey. *Historic American Buildings: California*. 4 vols. Introduction by David G. De Long. New York and London: Garland Publishing, 1980.

Jackson, Helen Hunt. *Ramona*. N.p.: Roberts Brothers, 1884.

Kirker, Harold G. *California's Architectural Frontier: Style and Tradition in the Nineteenth Century*. San Marino: Henry E. Huntington Library and Art Gallery, 1960; revised ed., Santa Barbara and Salt Lake City: Peregrine Smith, Inc., 1973.

May, Cliff. *Western Ranch Houses*. Menlo Park: Lane Magazine & Book Company, 1958.

Moyer, Cecil C. *Historic Ranchos of San Diego*. Edited and introduction by Richard E. Pourade. A Copley Book. San Diego: Union-Tribune Publishing Company, 1969.

Parks, Marion. "In Pursuit of Vanished Days: Visits to the Extant Adobe Houses of Los Angeles County, Part I," Historical Society of Southern California *Annual* XIV, no. 1, 1928, pp.6-63; Part II, XIV, no. 2, 1929, pp.134-207.

Pourade, Richard E. *The Silver Dons: The History of San Diego*. Historic Birthplace of California series, vol. 3. A Copley Book. San Diego: Union-Tribune Publishing Company, 1963.

Wilkes, Charles, U.S.N. *Narrative of the United States Exploring Expedition During the Years 1838, 1839, 1840, 1841, 1842*. Philadelphia: n.p., 1842.

Wilson, Florence Slocum. *Windows on Early California*. Foreword by W.W. Robinson. N.p.: The National Society of the Colonial Dames of America Resident in the State of California, Historical Activities Committee, n.d.; 1971.

closed as many as six distinct courts in a plan, with half walls and screens replacing full walls.

Cliff May's Los Angeles houses were enormously successful, due mainly to his ability to work unselfconsciously from memory rather than any effort to revive a past style. In a period when Modern was the reigning style, he did not hesitate to introduce purely pictorial features, but his selection of them was governed by the appro-

There were many other followers of the ranch house plan, some for tract housing, but the requirements of a generous site made the ranch house scheme too cramped for the typical tract. One architect, Quincy Jones, combined modernist design with many of the ranch house features in small houses on restricted sites by the use of interior courts. But the master of the ranch house revival continued to be Cliff May. He brought a sturdiness and an

opposite
Rancho Guajome,
San Diego, California, from 1851
left
Ranch house, Bel Air,
California, Cliff May, 1937

opposite
Barn, Pennsylvania
above, right
**Kwakiutl house,
Vancouver Island,
British Columbia**
above, left
**Sheet music for Our
Bungalow of Dreams,
1927**

For most of North America, through most of its history, wood has been the favored building material for houses; it still is, painted or natural, as frame or as surface or both. Wood is special stuff. Quite unlike steel or concrete, it was once alive. And though the tree doesn't continue to grow when it is cut down, its wood lives on; it can grow more beautiful with age if it is cared for, or it can (and probably will) curl and shrink and warp and crack and peel. For all its orneriness, it often works easily and is a satisfying substance for the sensitive craftsman, traditional or innovative.

We have a show of each: the "Plank House Architecture of the North West Coast Indians" describes a powerful tradition, now defunct, of red cedar plank houses of great beauty, charged with complex symbolism, where a rich tradition was the architect.

The other show about wooden houses, "The Common American Bungalow," is partly about tradition, but mostly about quick and even startling innovation, as the exotic one-story houses of Bengal (hence Bungalow) took root in Southern California, nourished by cheap land and good transportation (hence low density) and a climate as benign as its native one. It was built here in such prodigious numbers that it quickly came to be called the California Bungalow, and flourished in the hands of great architects, anonymous builders, and even ready-cut firms — innovation becoming almost instant tradition. The California bungalow, something over half a century ago, surrounded by its own lawn and gardens, stood for the good life, the American dream come true. To a remarkable degree it still does.
—P.B.

OR
WOOD

Bob Easton

THE PLANK HOUSE

*of the
Northwest Coast
Indians*[1]

And day came. Then [the boy] went out...he came to a big town. The fronts of all of the houses were painted. This was the Artisans' town. They took him to the chief's house, in the middle...And he was there ten days...they told him to learn the paintings on the fronts of the houses...[the chief] said to him, "They will tell you about a medicine."

From a Tsimshian myth recorded by J.R. Swanton

Traditional cultures are often appreciated for producing ingenious shelters uniquely responsive to climate and materials, though most of these shelters go well beyond the functional to symbolize their inhabitants' cosmology. Usually this meaning is not immediately apparent; it can be hidden or it can be a part of the structure itself. However, the natives of the Pacific Northwest Coast, inhabiting a region rich in natural resources, developed an architecture over a 10,000 year history that exuberantly expressed these usually unseen dimensions.

Elsewhere on the North American continent there were native houses of comparable ingenuity, size, and structural complexity, but nowhere else did they become such dynamic visual symbols of status, wealth, and myth as in the Northwest Coast plank house. The highly stylized animal figures carved or painted on both the exterior and interior served to integrate the house into the life of its inhabitants. That such monumental houses were built in a mild coastal climate zone strongly suggests the existence of a well developed architectural tradition shaped by complex cultural forces.

But is it architecture? Because primitive builders traditionally replicate a divine model, they are not architects in the Western sense. But if we expand the definition of architect to include tradition, then tradition, as the summation of a people's cultural history, becomes the architect.

Traditional architecture is inextricably linked in use and meaning to a people's entire cultural fabric. Environmental, economic, social, historical, and religious forces contribute to the shape of an architecture. When we study native cultures we must pay attention to the native point of view, which generally reveals a consciousness primarily influenced by oral tradition, myth, and common sense. Integrating these sometimes paradoxical elements into our investigations can complete the cultural equation, unlocking perceptions.

Significant photographic and written accounts as well as native oral accounts gathered by anthropologists and ethnographers in the 1800s provide the primary resource for studying traditional American

Indian architecture. None of the old plank houses are standing today; their abandoned cedar posts, beams and planks have rotted from decades of damp climate. The study of Northwest Coast Indian art and architecture is primarily possible because of the extensive work of anthropologist Franz Boas. Beginning in 1885, he visited the region 12 times and worked closely with Indian informant George Hunt. Boas recorded many aspects of Northwest Coast culture, including information about the houses and their uses, both secular and sacred. This data forms the basis for a case study of tradition as architect.

The narrow seacoast region of North America known as the Pacific Northwest Coast stretches from the mouth of the Columbia River in Oregon north to Yakutat Bay in southern Alaska. Geographically, it is a region of islands, fjords, sounds, and steep mountains that rise dramatically from the sea. The coastal climate is mild (35 degrees in winter to 60 degrees in summer), yet it is one of the wettest areas on earth, with rainfall of over 80 inches per year. At least 22 "tribes," of six language families, occupied the region. Northwest Coast "tribes" were not cohesive nations in any sort of political unity, but were groups of autonomous peoples who shared the same language and cultural details. Economically, the region is rich in natural resources; the sea providing plentiful salmon for food, the land providing forests of red cedar, an easily worked softwood that was the basic house building material.

Cedar logs stripped of bark became the structure of the post-and-beam house. Split cedar planks became house walls and roof. The resulting rectangular plank house was the typical house found throughout the region, varying in size and shape with local tradition.

Houses of chiefs and important families were decorated with images of sacred mythical animals by a special class of artisans. These decorations gave the house a special role within the culture. The visual display of family lineage, social status, and mythological and religious symbols provided social reinforcement.

The Indians had used woodworking tools made of stones and shells long before they had iron tools, which were acquired at first through trade with Siberia and later, in quantity, from white traders. These tools and the wealth that came with an increasing fur trade, allowed the building and carving arts to flourish during the 1800s. But it was this very contact with whites, which brought disease, alcoholism, and warfare, that led to a general dissolution of aboriginal Indian culture by the 1900s.

Exploration and discovery by Europeans was vigorous in the early contact period of 1778 to 1800. Traders returning from the remote Northwest Coast left written accounts of houses, villages, and life within them. Anthropologists, ethnographers, and photographers began collecting data in the late 1800s; the first photograph was taken in 1864.

The aboriginal origins of Northwest Coast culture have yet to be firmly established by archeological evidence. Anthropologist Philip Drucker in *Indians of Northwest Coast* hypothetically concludes that the source "...was a derivation of that of the ancient Eskimo." Eskimo use of planks would tend to verify these roots, and as to other sources, Drucker mentions "...In the Amur of Siberia region are found dwellings bearing...resemblance to the forms of the Northwest Coast," thus implying Asian roots. Plank houses are also found in northern Japan.

The plank house was built up and down the 1,200 miles of coast, but

93

NORTHWEST COAST TRIBES

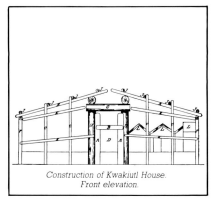

Construction of Kwakiutl House. Front elevation.

within South, Central, and Northern sub-regions, houses developed their own special architectural character. Plank houses varied as to size, shape, detail, and decoration, but universally had a structural system of post-and-beam frame with either a permanent or removable "skin" of wall and roof planks. Centuries of intertribal contact spread styles of building and art, altering and elaborating each tribe's archetypal modes. Dissemination contributed to individual differentiation and artistic expression, a behavior pattern uniquely acceptable on the Northwest Coast.

The southern sub-region, the home of the Salish-speaking people, extended from near the present-day Oregon-California border to the lower half of Vancouver Island. Their houses were usually undecorated and very long: there are early descriptions of shed houses almost 1,000 feet long and 60 feet wide. Consisting of many tribal subgroups, southern culture was fairly homogeneous. The extendable shed roof house was quite different in form (housing an extended family social structure) from those to the north, as it was usually bare of iconographic decorations. Planks were tied to the house frame (enabling them to be moved from permanent winter and summer house frames). They built smaller, gable roof structures after contact with the white man.

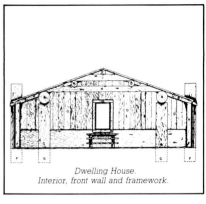

Dwelling House.
Interior, front wall and framework.

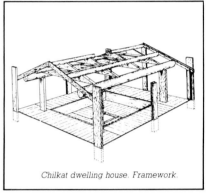

Chilkat dwelling house. Framework.

above, left
**Chief Klart Reech house,
Tlingit Village,
Chilkat, Alaska, 1895**
above, right, top
**Elevation: Interior, front
wall and framework,
Tlinglit-Chilkat house,
Alaska, 19th C**
above, right, bottom
**Framework, Tlinglit-
Chilkat house, Alaska,
19th C**
left
**Kwakiutl 2-beam house
frame, Memquimlees,
Vancouver Island, British
Columbia, ca 1917**

opposite, left
**Map, Northwest Coast
Tribes, 1936**
right, top
**Kwakiutl house,
Vancouver Island,
British Columbia**
right, bottom
**Front elevation, Kwakiutl
house, Vancouver Island,
British Columbia, ca 1900**

Large, rectangular gabled houses built around shallow pits sheltered the family groups of the Central sub-region. It was inhabited by three major groups: the Kwakiutl peoples lived mostly along the bays and inlets between the mainland and the eastern Vancouver Island coast; the Nootka lived on the harsh western coast; and the Mainland dwelling Bella Coola inhabited the mainland coast. Gable roof houses which were not extendable were the primary Central house type, featuring elaborately painted facades and carved interior posts and beams.

The North, a sub-region of more severe climate, was occupied by the "totem pole" building Lingit, Tsimshian, and Haida. Their houses had walls made of tightly fitted planks and elaborately carved structural elements. The art of carving here reached its highest expression. The houses of the Haida featured a different structural system than the typical two-beamed dwellings of the Central and other Northern tribes. Their six-beamed houses, clustered in villages along the beaches of the Queen Charlotte Islands, were pieces of monumental cabinetwork.

Throughout the entire coastal region, villages were usually comprised of a kinship group and were really autonomous political units,

claiming territory and acting independently. Settlements were always located near the water and were either permanent winter villages or temporary camps. They were sited on the seacoast, inlets, or rivers, as the thick forest necessitated travel by canoe. A typical village comprised two or three rows of houses lining a sheltered cove with a good beach for canoe access. The winter village, the permanent center of the seasonal settlement pattern of these semi-sedentary people, contained the large, permanent plank houses. Spring and summer village camps were collections of temporary shelters at fishing sites. Food for the winter was gathered at these camps by all able-bodied villagers. Those unable to contribute remained at the permanent village.

Northwest Coast people endowed the red cedar tree and its products with spiritual life. To the Kwakiutl the cedar was composed

of three vital parts. The cedar's outer bark was peeled, dried, shredded, and woven into blankets, ropes, mattresses, and garments. Its reddish hue symbolized cosmic blood, lending it *nawalak*, or supernatural force. The tree's second gift was its planks, which lost no spiritual power in their manufacture. Finally, an adzed cedar pole performed a pivotal function in winter ceremonies. Placed in the center of the floor and jutting 40 feet through the central smokehole, it linked house, sky, and underworld as *axis mundi*.

Red cedar is superb construction material: it is light and easily spilt; its oils retard rot and infestation. Previously, Boas was told, planks were split from driftwood logs, but in later times they were taken from standing or felled trees. Trees were carefully tested by "feeling into the tree," as the Kwakiutl phrased it, by making a hole with a long-handled chisel to determine

if the wood was sound. Coarse-grained wood was best for roof beams since it was most fire-resistant. House posts, rafters, and canoes called for the dense-grained wood found in aged trees with moss-covered trunks. Adzed cedar logs became the house's posts and beams; split planks, about 3 inches thick and sometimes over 3 feet wide, provided wall and roof. Final dimensions, joinery, profile, and decoration of beams and planks depended upon tribal style. An early visitor reported a Nootka carpenter's kit that contained iron tools, consisting of "...maul, chisels, wedges, D-adze, straight adze, simple drills, grindstones of sandstone for finishing, sharkskin for fine polishing...."

Northwest Coast architecture provided the prime mode for displaying personal station, prominence, and wealth. Boas learned that in Kwakiutl society the house did not belong to its living occupants but rather to the clan or lineage structure known as *numema*. Names and crests accrued to the house. Current dwellers were less owners than custodians of their lineage's property. The chief custodian of a localized group's possessions was the highest ranking member or chief. Acquisition of wealth to enhance the prestige of the lineage as well as one's own was a dominant incentive in Kwakiutl society and increased in importance with the fur trade. In the protocol of ostentatious display and generosity, the house played an important part as the stage for "potlatch" gatherings.

The term "potlatch," which comes from Chinook, means "giving." Secular potlatch ceremonies were public events to announce claims to privilege, commemoration of the dead, marriage, birth, the naming of a child, correction of social disgrace, repayment of loans, celebration of the erection or decoration of a house, and as a

The distribution of blankets, muskets &c at a grand distribution feast or pottack.

vehicle of competition between chiefs.

The most important function of the plank house, beyond its ability to provide shelter or display status, was as a symbol of the Indians' perception of the universe. Important houses acquired what were called "reputations." They were considered "beings," which incorporated past and present and remained on the site even when the structure was replaced. Winter was the sacred period of the year when the religious symbolism of the house came to life.

When the Haida house was hung with cedar boughs after a thorough cleaning, it was transformed from secular to sacred for the winter ceremonial season. Canadian anthropologist George MacDonald has compared the similarities of Haida cosmology to shamanistic beliefs found throughout the ancient world. He states that myth, and on the Northwest Coast, art, as it appears on the house structure, form part of an anthropo-cosmic equation, which Mircea Eliade calls the "Body-House-Cosmos." This conceptual equation describes the phenomena where the human/animal body is symbolized by man's house, his social and ritual structures, and the physical nature of his perceived universe.

Thus, the universe is seen as analogous to a living being; and is explained with images, or 'crests,' which are unique to each family's lineage and link them to their people, a supernatural treasure, constructed, decorated, and regarded in accord with mythological themes. The winter ceremonial dances would animate the house crests, as the dancers moved around the hearth/universe in the sun's direction, as if participating in the universe through their replication of its endlessly repeating cycles, with the sacred symbolic house/universe part of the cycle.

The most elaborate and structured ceremonial life was practiced by the Kwakiutl. Their ceremonies were full of drama, color, and special effects; the house became a theater. During dramatically staged ceremonials, lineage crest figures carved on interior house posts would sometimes be brought to life by similarly costumed dancers. Dancers would sometimes emerge from trap doors spewing feathers from intricately rigged masks. At these times, the house symbolically became the body of the cosmic ancestor: the houseposts, the limbs; the ridgepole, the backbone; the rafters, the ribs. The performing shaman thus brought to life the mythological motifs and cosmic worlds symbolized by the house.

Franz Boas never wrote a comprehensive work on his data concerning Northwest Coast ceremonial myths and religious life, but Irving Goldman, one of his many students to work with that data, attempted such a synthesis in his book, *The Mouth of Heaven*. Concentrating on Kwakiutl religious thought, he concludes "...They constructed a culture on their perception of natural phenomena and on their understanding of how the natural order works...drawing upon the unconscious resources of the mind, and upon its innate structures. In their desire to know the natural order and to understand their place within it, they are indeed the architects of their own destiny, and their culture is a personal and collective creation."

The plank house, in its sacred mode, was a cosmic container, with its own living force: the spirit incarnate of its inhabitants' ancestors. Beyond its secular function as shelter, its prime reason for existence was as a symbol of vital spatial and mythological concerns. It provided cultural continuity by being the sustaining tangible symbol of "place" for its inhabitants. Thus, the house, as said by the Kwakiutl, "...holding the tribe in its hands," stood as the prime symbol of culture.

Footnotes

1. Adapted from Peter Nabokov and Robert Easton, *Native American Architecture,* New York and Oxford: Oxford University Press, 1984.

opposite, left
Haida 6-beam house,
Haina, Queen Charlotte
Island, British Columbia,
late 1880s
right
Haida Village, Skidigate,
Queen Charlotte Island,
British Columbia, ca 1880

above
Potlatch ceremony, Salish
house, Old Songhees
Reserve near Victoria,
Vancouver Island,
ca 1867

Robert Winter

THE COMMON AMERICAN BUNGALOW

What is a bungalow? Definitions (perhaps conceptions is a better word) range so widely as to be completely mystifying. Sometimes it is simply another name for a cottage. Sometimes it refers to small one- or two-story residences set on the grounds of a large hotel. Sometimes it is a fairly easily discernible style based on elements of Swiss chalets and Japanese palaces and temples.

For the purpose of this exhibition the term will be used in its original sense to describe any basically one-story, free-standing, single-family dwelling built in the period 1880-1930. I hedge somewhat when I say "basically one-story"; the major characteristic of the bungalow was that it accommodated all the functions of living — recreation, dining, bathing, sleeping, preparing food, and eating — on one floor; still, from the first Queen Anne bungalow onward, there was a tendency to extend some of those functions, particularly sleeping, into the attic, which blossomed with dormers and windowed gables if only to house a guest room or a billiard table. But no house of a full two stories is a bungalow.[1]

As almost everyone knows, the term bungalow as well as the house type came from Bengal (modern Bangla-desh) where the word *bangla* refers to both the political region and the native dwelling, which generally consisted of a central family space surrounded by smaller rooms for sleeping and utilities. The British governors in Bengal adopted the style, but added ideas from the English cottage tradition, the Army tent, and other cultures to develop a house type for colonial administrators and western travellers. As early as 1793, the British version of the bangla had been developed to the point that its characteristics could be described in detail, by a Mr. William Hodges:

BEHIND THE BUNGALOW.
BY EHA,
AUTHOR OF "TRIBES ON MY FRONTIER."

WITH FIFTY-THREE CLEVER SKETCHES
By the Illustrator of "The Tribes."

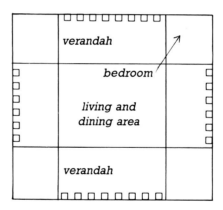

[Bungalows are] generally raised on a base of brick, one, two, or three feet from the ground, and consist of only one story; the plan of them usually is a large room in the centre for an eating and sitting room, and rooms at each corner for sleeping; the whole is covered with one general thatch, which comes low to each side; the spaces between the angle rooms are viranders [verandahs — the Persian word for porch] or open porticos to sit in during the evenings; the centre hall is lighted from the sides with windows and a large door in the centre. Sometimes the centre viranders at each end are converted into rooms.[2]

The bungalow spread throughout the tropical countries of the British Empire and, without the thatch, into other areas as well. Their simplicity and convenience made them adaptable to various uses — the lake or mountain cottage, the vacation home, and, by the end of the nineteenth century, the permanent home for millions of people in every flourishing city.

As Clay Lancaster has noted, the first mention of a bungalow being built in America was in the *American Architect and Building News* (1880).[3] It was for a cottage on Cape

Cod. The second reference was apparently in a little book by a New York architect, A.W. Brunner, *Cottages or Hints on Economical building* (1884) which illustrates "a bungalow with attic" by the author himself.[4] It is a Queen Anne cottage with dormers that allow additional sleeping space in the attic. With verandahs and a front door opening into the central hall or living room, the plan is more complex than the one described by William

motifs, but the underlying pattern for the bungalow and the style of life it permitted had been well established. The bungalow had begun in a native tradition and had been adapted to the recreational and administrative needs of British, Americans, and, in fact, almost every technologically advanced people in the world. It continued this function in many places, but what must interest us here is the manner in which this simple rural

Front Elevation

Side Elevation

BUNGALOW with ATTIC.

Plan

left
Perspective sketch, elevations and floor plan, Bungalow with Attic, Arnold W. Brunner, Cottages or Hints on Economical Building, *1884*

Perspective · Sketch of Bungalow
·Arnold·W·Brunner· Archt.
·····NEW·YORK·

Hodges in 1793, but it is, nevertheless, closely related to it. Even though designed by an architect, Brunner's cottage embodies a vernacular tradition of an essentially one-story, single-family dwelling, standing very importantly in a garden.

Almost twenty years elapsed between Brunner's essay in Queen Anne and the more familiar "Craftsman" bungalow that exhibited strong Oriental and Swiss Chalet

dwelling was altered to fit into an urban or suburban setting as well as the requirements of modern factory production.

The acres of bungalows in every American city and large town attest to the popularity of this house type in the first three decades of the twentieth century. In some ways it was least appropriate in the city, where high land prices mitigated against buildings that, being all on one floor, were the most extrava-

gant in the use of land. For this reason they were relegated to the suburbs where land prices were lower and where street-cars and then automobiles made the greater distances more practical.

In *The California Bungalow* (Hennessey & Ingalls, 1980) I argued that conditions in California, particularly in Southern California, met all the criteria for bungalow building — relatively cheap land and transportation that was inexpensive and efficient. In addition, Southern California provided a climate that made construction economies possible and encouraged the relationship between indoor and outdoor living that had been enjoyed in India. In fact, the conditions were so favorable for bungalows in California and so many enormous plantations of them were built here as a result that from Brooklyn to Vancouver to Sydney the Indian or the British or the American bungalow tended to be called a "California

bungalow."

Although the Eastern architectural establishment, led by the *Architectural Record*, generally frowned on the cheap dream-house as simply not architecture, the anti-establishment and the popular journals like *Good Housekeeping*, the *Ladies Home Journal*, and *House and Garden* took up the bungalow as a cause. Gustav Stickley's *Craftsman* magazine endorsed the style with enthusiasm and included many bungalows among its descriptions of Craftsman homes. *Keith's Magazine of Homebuilding*, published in Minneapolis, was a great champion of the bungalow and for years devoted its April issue to the subject with articles ranging from "A Bachelor's Bungalow" to "Rain on the Roof." Henry L. Wilson, whose *Bungalow Book* (1910) was one of the most stirring inspirations for the phenomenon, even founded a journal devoted wholly to the style, *Bungalow Magazine,* which

"THOSE WHO BUILD OF CYPRESS BUILD BUT ONCE."

HOME-BUILDING DAYS WILL BE HERE BEFORE YOU KNOW IT. LET'S BE READY.

HOME-BUILDING DAYS WILL BE HERE BEFORE YOU KNOW IT. LET'S BE READY.

Write us for the FREE PLANS to build this Cypress BUNGALOW.

Home Planning Time Is N-O-W!

Chilly days make the mental picture of a warm, cozy *"Home-of-our-Own"* a pleasant thought, and doubly so now that it is possible to bring these pleasant plannings to a happy reality, through the building of an "honest to goodness" house of genuine

"TIDE WATER" CYPRESS "THE WOOD ETERNAL"

under favorable building conditions.

If you are one of those who are indulging in the delightful occupation of home planning, will you let us help? Send TODAY for one of the very interesting

FREE BOOKS

of the internationally famous Cypress Pocket Library. In it you will find specifications and FULL-SIZE WORKING PLANS to build the "California bungalow" shown above. It was designed especially for us and our friends by one of America's cleverest architects, who knows how small homes should be. You will be delighted with it. The book also contains many excellent reasons why Cypress vitally affects the value of your building investment. Cypress "the Wood Eternal" reduces depreciation to the minimum. Write for **VOL. 18** today.

SOUTHERN CYPRESS MANUFACTURERS' ASSOCIATION
1225 Poydras Building, New Orleans, La., or 1225 Graham Building, Jacksonville, Fla.

 INSIST ON <u>TRADE-MARKED</u> CYPRESS AT YOUR LOCAL LUMBER DEALER'S. IF HE HASN'T IT, *LET US KNOW IMMEDIATELY.*

above
Advertisement,
Keith's Magazine,
March, 1923

opposite, left
Perspective and plan,
The Bungalow Book, *1910*
right
Perspective and plan,
Radford's Artistic
Bungalows, *1908*

he published first in Los Angeles and then in Seattle.

Many well-known architects designed bungalows. Charles and Henry Greene of Pasadena and Bernard Maybeck of Berkeley are the best known advocates on the West Coast. Frank Lloyd Wright not only designed and built bungalows, he devised a version that could be prefabricated. But here I am concerned only in passing with famous architects and beautiful design.[5] In this exhibition I have concentrated on what might be called "the common bungalow," which is not without style but suggests, even if it is eventually found to have an architect, that it has been designed by a committee with a desire to produce a floor plan and elevations that will provide respectability, if not fine art, for the prospective client.

For examples of the "common bungalow" I have gone to existing bungalow neighborhoods, but more often to the magazines that published plans and, especially, to the "bungalow books" put out by pattern book firms. The latter were meant to display a variety of elevations and floor plans from which a client might select the most suitable and then, for a fee of ten to twenty-five dollars, receive detailed plans from which a contractor could work. Some firms would, for a small additional fee, reverse a plan or even adapt it to the contours of the intended site.

These bungalow books were advertised in popular journals and, apparently, were handed out free of charge by contractors who were eager for jobs. In this way the bungalow-mania was fostered throughout the land. In fact, the dozens of such pattern books account for the surprising uniformity of bungalows throughout America as well as for the plentitude of them in every community that had even a moderate growth in the period just before and just after World War I.

Even greater contributors to the popularity of the bungalow were the "ready-cut" firms which promised enormous economies by prefabricating bungalows down to the finest detail of a built-in sideboard or a disappearing bed and by shipping these, carefully numbered and loaded, around the country so that a carpenter of even moderate skill could assemble them in a matter of days. The Aladdin Company of Bay City, Michigan, was one of the principal firms boasting "a complete home or a complete city." Sears-Roebuck catalogs advertised pre-fabricated bungalows as well as other houses. Los Angeles had at least two factories, California Ready-Cut and Pacific Ready-Cut. Davenport, Iowa, had its Gordon-Van Tine Plan-Cut Homes. The E.F. Hodgson Co., with addresses in Boston and New York, produced "portable" cottages and bungalows as well as "play houses, garages, dog kennels, poultry-houses, etc."

The common bungalow was not often up to the standards of the best Craftsman architects, but it offered a home with style to the American family of moderate means. Notable is the emphasis on the living room with its fireplace, often in an inglenook — important symbols of the sanctity of the family and the home in an age when these homey institutions were felt to be under attack. At the same time, the promoters emphasized that the bungalow must have all the latest conveniences of modern life, particularly in the bathroom, the kitchen, and the heating system. Surrounded by its own lawn and garden, the common American bungalow stood for the good life, the American Dream come true. It still does.

Footnotes

1. See Henry H. Saylor, *Bungalows,* Philadelphia: The John C. Winston Company, 1911, p.9.

Perspective View of No. 484.

The illustration opposite gives a good idea of the appearance of this half timber and stucco house, which has many characteristics of the English style of domestic architecture.

The main windows are of plate glass. Upon entering, the first point of interest is the ingle-nook; its stone mantel and seats are very carefully executed.

An auxiliary flight of stairs leading from the rear hall gives the advantage of a separate stairway in connection with the main stairway.

The corridor leading from living-room to dining-room is well lighted by the French doors opening upon the recessed side porch.

The dining-room located on the rear is a nearer approach to the European arrangement.

Two bed-rooms and a toilet-room are built upon the second floor. These could be utilized by the members of the family even though a servant be employed, as a maid's room is located on the rear screen porch.

The main body of this house is 36 feet in width; add 4 feet for the rear toilet-room. The length is 56½ feet, to which is added 8½ feet by the maid's room, and 7 feet by the additional projection of the front porch. It could be built for $3,300.

Complete plans and specifications of this house with all necessary details, either as shown on this page or reversed, will be furnished for $10.00.

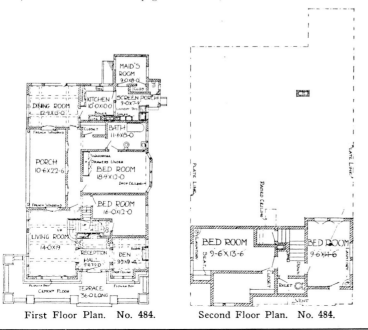

First Floor Plan. No. 484.   Second Floor Plan. No. 484.

Design No. 5039

Size: Width, 24 feet; Length, 58 feet 6 inches

Blue prints consist of basement plan; floor plan; front, rear, two side elevations; wall sections and all necessary interior details. Specifications consist of twenty-two pages of typewritten matter.

PRICE

of Blue Prints, together with a complete set of typewritten specifications

ONLY

$10.00

We mail Plans and Specifications the same day order is received.

Floor Plan

133

2. Quoted by Anothony King in his "The Bungalow: An Indian Contribution to the West," *History Today,* 32, November 1982, p.39.

3. Clay Lancaster, "The American Bungalow," *Art Bulletin,* 40, 1958, p.239.

4. A.W. Brunner, ed., *Cottages or Hints on Economical Building,* New York: William T. Comstock, 1884.

5. For descriptions of some of the most beautiful of the bungalow breed, see: Robert Winter, *The California Bungalow,* Los Angeles: Hennessey & Ingalls, 1980.

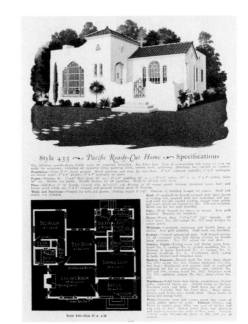

Style 435 ~ Pacific Ready-Cut Home ~ Specifications

Style 435—Size 27-6 x 32

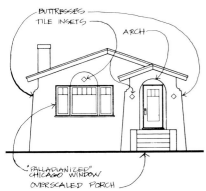

BUTTRESSES
TILE INSETS
ARCH
"PALLADIANIZED"
CHICAGO WINDOW
OVERSCALED PORCH

opposite
Detail, house,
Oakland, California
above, top
House, Los Angeles,
California, 1960
above, bottom
Typical Eclectic Stucco *house*
right
Perspective and plan,
Pacific Book of Homes,
1925

Stucco is a chameleon of a building material, marvelously adaptive, versatile, cheap, and capable of speaking in many voices without entirely laying to rest the suspicion that none of the voices is its own. Stucco is, after all, a covering material, which can be spread upon wood frame or masonry or steel or concrete. It can stretch across a thin wood frame of the proper shape to resemble a thrillingly plastic mass, perhaps redolent of old Spain, or at least its Colonial extensions. David Gebhard, in the first of the three exhibitions described in this section, mounts a study of the stucco box become, with confident massing and a very few ebullient details, the Mediterranean, or Spanish Colonial Revival version of the American Dream. He makes it seem a highly desirable one.

Another version of the stucco skin again stretches over a frame, usually of wood, to make the crisp and unadorned, interlocked rectangular solids that were a central vision of the International Style. There are some finely wrought, architect-designed versions in Southern California, which have been in enough history books to be classifiable as High Art. But there are many many more anonymous ones: "Eclectic Stucco" is centered on Oakland in the '20s, when the choices among ornamental vocabularies were wide. "The Stucco Box," on the other hand, concentrates on the speculative stucco-faced apartment houses in Los Angeles of the years from 1954 until the end of the '50s, when a change in zoning and parking requirements spelled their doom, and a bigger and uglier format was mandated. Many were built, so they qualify as vernacular in one of the stricter senses of that word we are playing so fast and loose with.
—P.B.

OR
COVERED
WITH
STUCCO

David Gebhard

TILE, STUCCO WALLS AND ARCHES:

The Spanish Tradition in the Popular American House

"A dominant element in the growing popularity of Spanish architecture is the appeal which it so often makes to that sense of the noble and the enduring...its wrought iron grills and other details that recall the days of mystery." So wrote Margaret Craig in the December, 1922 issue of the widely read *Keith's Home Magazine*.[1] Over the years modernist architects of high seriousness and their apologists have been uneasy about the recurring popularity of the Spanish image. Paul Edgar Murphy, writing in the April, 1928, *American Mercury,* summed up these reservations when he wrote of the current architectural scene in California: "If a house has its exterior covered with stucco, it is Spanish. If its stucco appears to have been battered with an elephant's foot, or trowelled to resemble a waffle-iron, it is more Spanish. If it has a tile roof, or even a tile eyebrow along the coping, it is yet more Spanish. If the builder has added a window awning supported on spears, it has reached the zenith."[2]

Murphy and others before and after were not objecting to the earlier usage of the Mission Revival image or the then current Spanish (Hispanic) image of the '20s. What they were flaying at was the very idea of middle-class dreams being realized through middle-class speculative housing. "The retired self-made man from the Corn Belt comes to California, sees the Mission Plays, reads *Ramona,* and must straightway build him a Spanish house."[3] Though no one would question that the most enduring image for speculative housing in America has been and is the Eastern Colonial, still no architectural image can compete with the Spanish for suggesting the romanticism of the far distant and far away in time. Popular as well as high art Spanish architecture has been maneuvered to suggest the provincialism of geographic regions, as has been the case over the decades in California and Florida. But the Spanish image has, since the late nineteenth century, been used to intimate that we can walk back and forth through the barrier that separates the fable of the past from the actuality of the moment. In an article "Castles in Spain," Marion Brownfield observed that the desire to create one's own "castle" is close to universal and that no image better suits this need than that of a "Spanish castle."[4]

The Spanish image as "...a vivid style with a romantic history" was, like other borrowings of the late nineteenth and early twentieth centuries, anything but pure.[5] The language was continually enriched by reminiscences of the Moorish architecture of Spain and North Africa, of Italian architecture, of that of Mexico, of the adobe traditions of the American Southwest and, from the '20s on, by the Anglo

Style 435 ∼ *Pacific Ready-Cut Home* ∼ Specifications

The following specifications briefly cover the materials furnished. See Price List. Cost of constructing this home on your lot ready for occupancy, including all carpenter labor, painting labor, cement work, plastering, plumbing, etc., quoted on request.
Foundation—Floor 2'-0" above ground. Wood platform and steps for rear door. 2" x 6" redwood mudsills; 2" x 4" underpins on outside walls; 4" x 4" girders; 4" x 4" underpins on piers.
Frame—Douglas fir. 2" x 6" floor joists 16" o.c.; 2" x 4" studding 16" o. c.; 2" x 4" rafters 24" o. c.; 2" x 4" ceiling joists 16" o.c. Double top plates. Double headers for all openings. Hood in kitchen over stove.
Floor—Sub-floor 1" fir boards covered with ⅜" x 1½" oak flooring in all rooms except kitchen, breakfast nook, bath and screen porch which are 1" x 4" tongued and grooved vertical grain fir flooring.
Walls and Partitions—Framed for lath and plaster. Ceiling height 8'-3⅞". Outside of building framed for stucco. Staff and stucco not included.

Roof—1" surfaced fir boards covered with three layers of roofing felt, mopped with hot asphaltum and covered with two-ply sanded roofing, except front gables and tower which are framed for tile. Tile not included. Metal cap for fire wall included.
Patio—Walls framed for stucco as shown. Iron grill included. Masonry not included.
Doors—Front door 3'-0" x 7'-0" 1¾" Special. All other doors No. 205 except No. 303 from kitchen to screen porch.
Windows—Casement, stationary and double hung as shown. Iron grill included. Staff work not included.
Screens—14-mesh galvanized wire. Full hinged screens for all casement sash, half sliding screens for double hung windows. No. 551 screen for rear door.
Interior Finish—Living room and dining room baseboard No. 3; casings No. 6; picture moulding No. 3. Balance of house baseboard No. 1; casings No. 1; picture moulding No. 3. Continuous head casing in bath, kitchen and breakfast nook.
Built-in Features—Mantel shelf No. 912; linen closet No. 501; cooler No. 402; kitchen cupboard No. 208, two door; drainboard and counter shelf of cupboard prepared for tile or composition; sink cabinets No. 303 and 304; ironing board No. 1022; breakfast nook No. 703; medicine cabinet No. 603; china closet No. 206.
Hardware—Solid brass door knobs, escutcheons, drawer pulls, cupboard turns, etc. Nickel finish in kitchen, breakfast nook and bath. Dull brass for all other rooms. Cylinder lock for front door. Door butts, hinges, sash locks, etc., plated steel. Glass knobs in living and dining room.
Print—Exterior trim and screen porch two coats of paint, either white or color. Interior—Floors, oak floors to receive paste filler, one coat of shellac and one coat of wax. Screen porch floor, rear platform and steps to receive two coats of floor paint. Interior —Four coats throughout, three of flat and one of enamel.

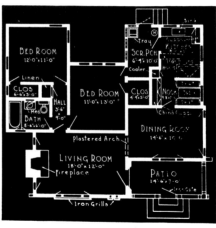

Style 435—Size 37 -6 x 32

traditions of the Monterey Style and of the Colonial of the American East. Roy Hilton, one of California's publishers of stock plans and pattern books, wrote that those promoting the Spanish image had "...gone back to Spain for fundamentals but they have not hesitated to avail themselves of other principles to service their purpose in creating homes of beauty."[6]

In California and Florida the rationale for employing the Mission and Spanish idiom was in part an outcome of the desire to set these two geographical areas apart from the rest of the United States. In each case, an entire geographic region was eventually viewed as a design object — an entire landscape to be created in a new historical image. But whether a new city or simply a single spec house, comments and observations were continually reported that went a long way to explain what the Spanish forms meant for the middle-class American audience. As with all historic architectural languages, the desire was to conjure reminiscences. Gustav Stickley, the preeminent figure of the turn-of-the-century Arts and Crafts movement in America, opened his 1909 volume *Craftsman Homes* with a Spanish design, of which he notes: "It was only natural that our first expression of this idea (the idea of Craftsman architecture) teenth century was derived from literary images. The popular nineteenth-century American author Washington Irving painted a beautifully vivid word picture of Spanish Moorish architecture in his 1832 *The Alhambra*. Of his stay in the Alhambra, Irving wrote: "Behold for once a day-dream realized; yet I can scarce credit my senses, or believe that I do indeed inhabit the palace of Boabdil, and look down from its balconies upon chivalric

should take shape in a house which, without being exactly founded on the Mission architecture so much used in California, is nevertheless *reminiscent* of that style..."[7] And as late as 1941, Phillip L. Pritchard, another of Los Angeles's virtual army of publishers of pattern books, asserted in the caption for one of his Hispanic designs that it was "Reminiscent of the California Missions."[8] Other designs ranged through time and place — from "a house design from Old Mexico suggestive of the Cliff Dwellers" to a Crane Company bathroom of the '20s that was "transplanted from an estancia in old Seville...this bathroom is as Spanish as the sharp click of castanets."[9]

These Spanish reminiscences were, of course, not from firsthand past experience, but were indirect — and being indirect they became more abstract and looser. The first inkling of the Hispanic in the nine-

opposite
**Perspective and plan,
Pacific Book of Homes,
1925**

left
**Advertisement,
House Beautiful,
April, 1928**
above
**Craftsman house in
California Mission style,
Craftsman Homes, 1909**

Shrewesbury's Beautiful Homes

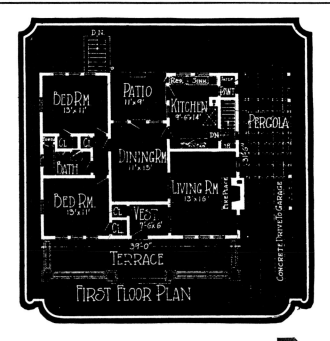

DISTINCTIVE SPANISH BUNGALOW WITH A PATIO.
For those who prefer the Spanish style of architecture this 5-room home of economical cost should greatly appeal. While it reminds one of the quaint old Spanish missions, it still retains the delightful atmosphere and room arrangement of modern American bungalows. The walls are of stucco and the Spanish features, the flat roof, the protruding beams, the red tiled canopy, the pergola and the patio have all been designed and worked in attractively, giving both exterior and interior a pleasing appearance. Price. **$4,225**

The play between the reality of the moment and the suggestiveness of the past, which is the essence of Irving's romantic response to Moorish Spain, was nurtured and continued on into this century. A 1930 advertisement of the Morgan Woodwork Organization expressed a similar sentiment: "There is a bit of the romanticist in all of us that responds instantly to the unique fascination found only in houses of Spanish design...they breathe romance."[11] An American of the '20s might not be able "...to live one's life out" in a whitewashed, iron balconied house in the Andalusian Spanish city of Ronda, but one could dwell in suburbia in a $4,200 spec "Spanish type bungalow...as carried to the Pacific Coast by the early Spanish residents."[12]

The visual language of Spain, far distant and deeply immersed in the reality of the European and American fairy tale, was heightened by what was written and said about the modest American Hispanic house. Instead of describing the small spec houses as simply Spanish, they were, following a time-honored nineteenth-century custom, provided with suggestive names. *The American Builder's* 1925 models mustered such names as "The Alvarado" and "The Alamonte"; in Charles Lane Bowes's *Book of Designs,* five rooms, bath, and garage were presented as "The Auricula." One need not know that "Giralda" referred to the twelfth-century Moorish minaret tower of the Cathedral of Seville; nor was it at all essential that the viewer had read William H. Prescott's *History of the Conquest of Mexico* to respond to Finzer Brothers Clay Company's design "The Cortez," with its arched entrance, awninged terrace, and the "gleaming red" of its tile roof.[13] A post-World War II four-room bungalow with its tile roof, chimneys with clay pots, and wood shutters with cut-outs of hearts was enriched by its name "Siesta"; and a simple stucco single family cottage in *A Place to Hang Your Heart* was called "Senorita," so that its Hispanic origins were unmistakable.[14]

"The magic of Spain — only three little words but how potent!"; Esther Matson in the September, 1923, issue of *Keith's Magazine* went on to describe how "the spell of Spain" had become a fact "...not only in fancy but in brick and mortar, or more literally speaking in this case, tile and stucco..."[15] She noted two qualities that were essential to the Spanish: the fundamental principle of art known as "Contrast," and the cultivation of the "picturesque." The Spanish mode, she wrote, was a highly "expressive" image which could convey the needs and tastes of the individual. Like others before and after, she spoke of the "magic glamor of romance" that was at the heart of the Hispanic image.[16] The author of the 1921 pattern book *Building With Assurance* presented a "Spanish" plan No. 18, with the remark, "...no other style of architecture offers such opportunities for the expression of individuality"; and the Morgan Woodwork Organization commented that the style offered the designer and woodworker "...characteristic forms of distinct individuality which contain in them also something of our own national spirit."[17] Individuality could come about by the picturesque ensemble of forms and details. Discussions of the Spanish image often mentioned its "festal character"; one's dwelling should not only be utilitarian, but an example of "good taste"; it should also have a quality of gaiety about it.[18] From its inception, with the Mission Revival, the Hispanic had been used for a broad range of recreational buildings — from park structures to amusement parks. And that quality of the Spanish, as a symbol

of out-of-doors, of sunshine and play, was continually alluded to, especially during the decade of the 1920s.

The Spanish also had other advantages that were continually pointed out. "Few conventions bind it and its plasticity — its susceptibility to varying treatment..." was one of its often mentioned and appealing qualities.[19] And, as was the case with all Revivalist architecture, the spec builder and the publishers of pattern books emphasized that a home buyer could have his cake and eat it too. The dwelling could be both modern in plan, materials, and structure, and picturesque in character. The Oklahoma City architect William H. Schumacher captioned one of his 1938 Spanish designs: "This one story Spanish House is one that is practical, and meets modern requirements, yet retaining or reflecting much of the old world charm."[20] Always, the historic image was accompanied by a comment as to the modernity (and practicality) of its design. "This distinctive house of Mediterranean origin is," noted the caption for Design No. 5-B-6 in *Correctly Designed Spanish Homes* of 1930, "an excellent example of a house planned and designed to suit modern requirements. Simple in outline and romantic in character, it will strongly appeal to the builder who looks for individuality in his home."[21]

The flexibility of approach taken to the design of an Hispanic house was reflected in its structure and materials, in its siting, in its planning, and in its willing delight to incorporate other images. This has meant that the mode has always tended to be associated with whatever was considered to be "modern" at the moment. At the turn of the century the Mission Revival cottage, with its bungalow plan, fumed oak woodwork, clinker bricks, and boulder fireplaces, was readily embraced by the Craftsman Arts

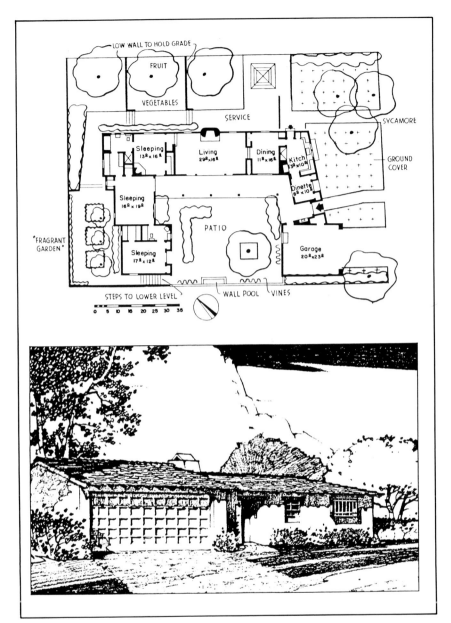

and Crafts movement. In the 1920s, the Spanish Mediterranean image was seen as something very close to the newly evolving popular Moderne (Art Deco), and the elitist International Style. In the '30s, the California Ranch Houses of Cliff May, William W. Wurster, and H. Roy Kelley were seen as gentle domesticated versions of the Modern. And the numerous variations on the Spanish theme, which have continued in spec housing to this

opposite
Perspective and plan, Spanish Bungalow, Shrewesbury's House Plans, *1924*

above
California Ranch House, Cliff May, Sunset Western Ranch Houses, *1946*

day, are consistently seen as being both modern and romantic.

Each of the decades in which the Spanish image has been employed has developed its own individual version of the language, providing a readable image addressed to the middle class. The vocabulary of the Mission image was keyed to four ingredients: stucco walls, arched openings, parapeted end gables, and tile roofs. The more elaborate examples enriched this experience by adding quatrefoil windows, occasional ogee and cusped Moorish arches, and single or paired towers. In plan these Mission houses and bungalows were identical to Craftsman and late Queen Anne designs of the period — with the exception that they occasionally were centered around partially enclosed patios and parapeted and pergola covered terraces. A favored spec and pattern book type was that of an H-shaped grouping of rooms — with an entrance courtyard toward the street and a patio-terrace to the rear. Ye Planry Building Company of Los Angeles's 1908 design No. 331, "...carries out the fundamental bungalow idea of grouping rooms about a central room."[22]

The image of the Mission could be suggested by a minimum of elements, as was pointed out in the 1922 *Minneapolis Tribune Plan Book for Home Builders,* where 'a "Spanish Mission Bungalow" was realized "...by the curved lines of the gable end and the tile detailing of the main roof and the sun porch roof, worked out by a special method of laying red asphalt shingles."[23] The patio, as a symbol of Mission and later of the Spanish mode, was often dealt with by intimation rather than fact — and that as a symbol was all that was necessary. In Plan No. 354 in *The Book of a Thousand Homes* of 1921, we enter a Spanish bungalow "...via an open patio through a wooden gate," and

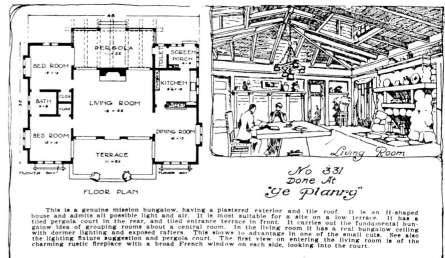

FLOOR PLAN

No 331
Done At
"Ye Planry"

This is a genuine mission bungalow, having a plastered exterior and tile roof. It is an H-shaped house and admits all possible light and air. It is most suitable for a site on a low terrace. It has a tiled pergola court in the rear, and tiled entrance terrace in front. It carries out the fundamental bungalow idea of grouping rooms about a central room. In the living room it has a real bungalow ceiling with dormer lighting and exposed rafters. This shows to advantage in one of the small cuts. See also the lighting fixture suggestion and pergola court. The first view on entering the living room is of the charming rustic fireplace with a broad French window on each side, looking into the court.

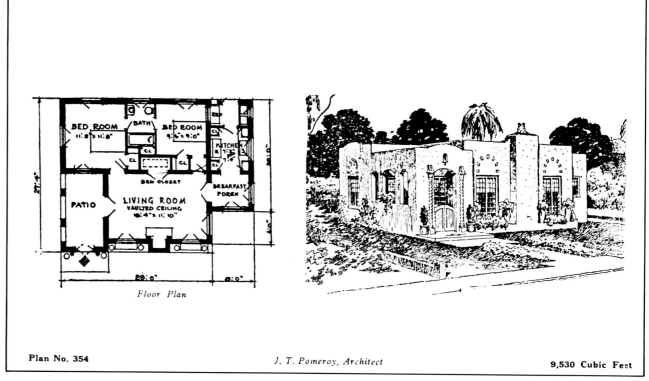

Floor Plan

Plan No. 354   *J. T. Pomeroy, Architect*   **9,530 Cubic Feet**

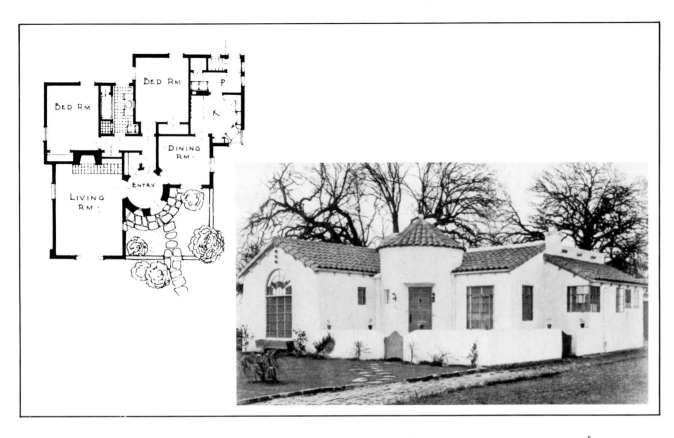

opposite, right, top
Interior perspective and plan, Mission bungalow, Ye Planary Bungalows, *1908*
left
Spanish Mission bungalow, The Minneapolis Tribune Plan Book for Home Builders, *1922*
right, bottom
Perspective and plan, Spanish Mission style bungalow, J.T. Pomeroy, The Book of A Thousand Homes, *1921*
left
A snug Spanish Bungalow and plan, Inspiration Homes, *1938*
below
"Casa Hermosa del oeste dorado," New Spanish Bungalows, *1926*

"...find ourselves in a walled enclosure open to the sky."[24] As the Hispanic image gradually eased into the Spanish Colonial Revival of the 1920s, the builders often repeated room-in-a-line Craftsman bungalow plans — transformed the narrow porch or pergola off the living and dining rooms into a patio with a low stucco wall broken by a wrought iron gate and a tile floor; and this, together with a few arches and a touch of tile roofing, made the dwelling Hispanic. Through the '20s and '30s, low walls, hedges, the placement of the garage, and the occasional irregularities of plan were used to create the impression of the Spanish patio.

As with the bungalow, the two-story pattern book spec Spanish house more often than not carried on traditional, highly workable plans. A white-painted brick dwelling of 1936, published in the Northwest Lumberman's Association's *Practical Small Homes,* is that of the much favored compact, efficient side hall plan, while Boston's Beamy-Slab "Design for a 7 Room House" carries on the equally functional central hall scheme.[25] Especially in the '20s, the picturesque nature of the exterior was appreciably enhanced by projecting a story-and-a-half living room off the two-story volume of the house — with the result that playful balconies or scarf-draped windows opening off a stair landing or an upstair's hall made it possible to peek secretly down on the activities below. Towers, both circular and square, were a builder's delight, and since the house was often entered through a door at the base of the tower, the castle image was strengthened further.

The '30s and the years following were in their own way as inventive in the maneuvering of the Hispanic image as before. The Spanish was merged into the American Colonial to produce the Monterey Revival

Style; it was mixed into the California Anglo, late nineteenth-century rural board-and-batten to emerge as the California Ranch House; and in the hands of many designers of spec houses and pattern book plans, it was made new, fashionable, and contemporaneous, by bringing in elements of the then popular Streamline Moderne (sometimes hinting at the delicate formalism of the Regency). In the 1936 Portland Cement Association's *Design for Concrete,* John Floyd Yewell's two-story scheme played a wide field: below its Monterey balcony was a panel of Modern glass bricks; to the rear, the glass-walled living and dining spaces opened onto a wide and partially enclosed terrace.[26] And in the Bank of America's *Inspiration Homes* of 1938, a "Snug Spanish Bungalow" exhibits another hallmark of the Moderne: a steel casement corner window.[27]

In the post-World War II years, the California Ranch House was seized upon by the American middle class as *the* popular dwelling for suburban spec housing. Though the pre-1940 sources of this image varied, its principal exponent was the Los Angeles designer Cliff May. He, along with the staff of the popular *Sunset* magazine, propagandized the California Ranch House across America. In their 1946 volume, *Sunset Western Ranch Houses,* they wrote: "The form called a ranch house has many roots. They go deep into Western soil. Some feed directly on the Spanish period. Some draw upon the pioneer years. But the ranch house growth has never been limited to its roots. It has never known a set style. It was shaped by needs for a special way of living — informal, yet gracious."[28]

Even the rage of the late '50s and '60s for the suburban split-level was susceptible to Spanishization. As early as 1938, the Millbrae High lands Company was offering the "Vista Superba," a split-level with an exterior patio, balcony, and tile roof that recalled the "Days of the Dons."[29] The more opulent spec houses of the late '60s and early '70s, with their double or triple car garages, their three to four baths, carried on the Spanish version of the split-level theme. Science and Mechanics Publishing Company of New York, in their 1969 Spring/Summer edition of *101 Home Plans,* offered blueprints and specifications for a "Spanish split-level" that provided the atmosphere of "dramatic living."[30] While the first of the spec condominiums of the '60s reflected the Third Bay Tradition of Charles Moore and others, Spanish "respectability" and historical roots remained. Thus, in the early 1980s, the advertisements for the "Villa de Malaga Town Homes" in Santa Monica captured "the Charming Architecture of Malaga, Spain..." with "authentic details such as hand-painted tiles on your front steps; fountains; wrought iron; beautiful flower pots."[31]

In a sense the Hispanic image has provided the same atmosphere of continuity of tradition that the East Coast Colonial has entailed for America east of the Mississippi. The close-to-one-hundred year usage of the Spanish idiom has remained to this day as a remarkably alive architectural language. Its success, like other continuously recurring architectural images, has been due to its plasticity. E.M. Oren noted this quality in discussing two designs, "Capistrano" and "El Ranchito" in the pages of the February, 1927 issue of the *California Home Owner:* "Liberties have been taken here with conventional Spanish design, but liberties taken with convention by sensitive artists have marked the progress of all art forms from age to age. Any captious critic might hurl all the precedent in half of Spain, with the Balearic Islands thrown in, without distracting so much as a jot from the effective charm of the plan or the perspective."[32]

Over the decades the Hispanic theme of tile, stucco walls, and arches has effectively evoked that human quality labeled "charm," a quality that has seldom been realized in the many images of the modern in this century. The emotive feeling of charm is rooted in tradition, as the designers of spec houses and pattern book plans fully realized. "Simplicity of detail in the Spanish house is a principal factor in producing that feeling of substantiality which is a dominant and worthwhile characteristic of any home."[33] And simplicity in the Spanish connoted a rural scene of the past, not that of the machine or hygiene. "There are many ways," wrote Marion Brownfield, "to contrive a 'Spanish castle,'" and the streets of America's suburbias aptly attest to its continued success.[34]

opposite
"Villa de Malaga Townhomes,"
The Los Angeles Times,
August 22, 1982

right
Details, houses, Los Angeles, California

Footnotes

1. Margaret Craig, "Spanish Influence," *Keith's Home Magazine,* vol. 48, December 1922, p.3.

2. Paul Edgar Murphy, "Native Architecture in Southern California," *American Mercury,* vol. 13, April 1928, p.450.

3. Murphy, "Native Architecture," p.450.

4. Marion Brownfield, "Castles in Spain," *Keith's Magazine,* vol. 51, June 1924, pp.279-81.

5. Architects' Small House Service Bureau, *How to Plan, Finance and Build Your Home,* Minneapolis: Architects' Small House Service Bureau, 1921, p.43.

6. Roy Hilton, *Spanish Homes of California,* Long Beach: The Roy Hilton Company, 1925, p.3.

7. Gustav Stickley, *Craftsman Homes,* New York: The Craftsman Publishing Company, 1909, p.9.

8. Phillip L. Pritchard, *California Small Homes,* Los Angeles: Architectural Book Shop, 1941, p.29.

9. *Homes and Fireside,* n.p.: n.p., 1926; advertisement by the Crane Company, *House Beautiful,* vol. 113, April 1928, p.413.

10. Washington Irving, *The Alhambra,* New York: The MacMillan Co., 1922 (first published in 1832), p.50.

11. The Architects' Small House Service Service Bureau, Morgan Woodwork Organization Co-operating, *Correctly Designed Spanish Homes,* Oshkosh, Wisconsin: The Architects' Small House Service Bureau, Morgan Woodwork Organization Co-operating, 1930, p.14.

12. Eleanor Elsner, *Spanish Sunshine,* New York: The Century Co., 1925, p.128; Shrewesbury Publishing Company, *Shrewesbury's House Plans,* Chicago: Shrewesbury Publishing Company, 1924, p.53.

13. Economy Planning Service, Inc., *Real Homes of Character and Distinction,* West Palm Beach, Florida: Economy Planning Service, Inc., 1927, pp.16-17; The Finzer Brothers Clay Company, *Beauty in Brick,* Sugar Creek, Ohio: The Finzer Brothers Clay Company, 1931, p.45.

14. Home Builders' Research Institute, Inc., *A Place to Hang Your Heart,* Washington, D.C.: Home Builders' Research Institute, 1946, n.p..

15. Esther Matson, "The Magic of Spain: On Wall, Window and Balcony," *Keith's Magazine,* vol. 50, September 1923, p.103.

16. Matson, "Magic," p.106.

17. Morgan Woodwork Organization, *Building With Assurance,* Oshkosh, Wisconsin, Morgan Woodwork Organization, 1921, p.41; Small House Service, *Spanish Homes,* p.2.

18. "The Three Best Homes of Tacoma, Washington," *House Beautiful,* vol. 49, January 1921, p.16.

19. Roy Hilton, *Spanish Homes of California,* Long Beach: The Roy Hilton Company, 1925, p.3.

20. William H. Schumacher, *A New Book of Distinctive Houses,* Oklahoma City: Distinctive Books Publishers, 1938, design No.41.

21. Small House Service, *Spanish Homes,* p.9.

22. Ye Planry Building Company, Inc., *Ye Planry Bungalows,* Los Angeles: Ye Planry Building Company, Inc., 1908, p.63.

23. The Minneapolis Tribune, *The Minneapolis Tribune Plan Book for Home Builders,* Minneapolis: The Minneapolis Tribune Co., 1922, design No.611.

24. Henry Atterbury Smith (compiler), *The Book of a Thousand Homes,* New York: Home Owners Service Institute, 1921, p.147.

25. Northwestern Lumbermen's Ass'n., *Practical Small Homes,* Third Edition, Minneapolis: Northwestern Lumbermen's Ass'n., 1936, p.7; Housing Company, *Beamy-Slab Houses,* Boston: Housing Company, 1927, p.15.

26. Portland Cement Association, *Designs for Concrete,* Chicago: Portland Cement Association, 1936, p.4.

27. Bank of America, *Inspiration Homes Built by Californians,* San Francisco: Bank of America, 1938, p.2.

28. Cliff May and The Editorial Staff of Sunset Magazine, *Sunset Western Ranch Houses,* San Francisco: Lane Publishing Co., 1946, *ix.*

29. Francis W. Brown, Editor and Publisher, *California Homes Plan Book 1939,* San Francisco and Los Angeles: California Homes Publishing Company, 1939, p.83.

30. Dick Demske, Editor, *101 Home Plans, Spring/Summer Edition,* New York: Science and Mechanics Publishing Company, 1969, Plan No.p-941.

31. Advertisement for the "Villa de Malaga Townhouses," offered by the California Development Corp., *Los Angeles Times,* August 22, 1982, part VIII, p.15.

32. E.M. Oren, "Two Houses of Spanish Precedent," *California Home Owner,* vol. 5, February 1927, pp.10, 11, 13.

33. Manila Seaver, "Spanish and Substantial," *California Home Owner,* vol. IV, June 1926, p.11.

34. Marion Brownfield, "Castles in Spain," *Keith's Magazine,* vol. 51, June 1924, p.280.

Kirk E. Peterson

ECLECTIC STUCCO

The southwestern United States, primarily California, is the location of a vernacular architecture, mainly homes, that uses the building material stucco to create a neutral box to which is added a variety of design elements from classical to Modern. The bold, chunky masses of these buildings, which in California make up whole districts of cities, are artifacts of an increasingly urban, industrial, and culturally diverse society. For the most part, they were constructed neither by owner/occupants, as in simpler societies, nor by the traditional system of clients and architects; most were built for the popular market by speculative builders, who designed the buildings themselves, generally unaware of any high art sources. These sources, though, are evident; usually a blend of two widespread trends: the historical (primarily Mediterranean and classical) and the progressive (primarily the Prairie School and the Arts and Crafts).

Toward the turn of the century, the people of California and the Southwest began to grow conscious of their region's special cultural heritage and began, moreover, to cultivate that consciousness. From this awareness grew a uniquely Southwestern way of life, called later by some the "California Good Life," which was exemplified and helped along by a number of widely popular publications, most notable of which was *Sunset, the Magazine of Western Living.* California was seen and promoted by its inhabitants as a place free of the traditions that bound other parts of the nation from which many Californians had emigrated. In the West, progressive ideas could take root in many aspects of culture including architecture. Writers, such as Mary Austin and Ernest Peixotto, eulogized the lovely land and climate of California, which recalled for them the lands of Mediterranean antiquity and hinted at an ap-propriate architecture. Simultaneously, the Arts and Crafts movement had discovered the West. The *Craftsman Magazine* declared, "In the West, where man not only dares to be honest but is encouraged in every way to express himself, there has arisen a simpler and more honest architecture."[1]

And so these buildings evolved, a blend of traditional and modern elements in a mutual celebration of the Southwest. The result generally looks at home in a regional landscape that has a romantic or even a classical Arcadian quality. Herbert Hoover, in reference to his own stucco house, speaks of a "blend of fine living and the new spirit of native western architecture."[2] Both the sense of history and the "new spirit" can be seen in the forward-looking work of talented architects like Irving Gill, Louis Christian Mullgardt, John Hudson Thomas, and even of less

proficient designers like Henry Trost and the Wolfe brothers. Yet the body of work produced by these men was relatively small. It is in the realm of the vernacular, in the speculative buildings done by non-professional designers, that there begins to emerge a "California tradition of startling combinations of diverse architectural images."[3]

In the early part of the century, and especially in the 1920s, a booming economy brought tremendous waves of immigrants to California and, with them, a great demand for moderately priced housing. Builders answered the call with duplexes and four-plexes and with houses in vast tracts; to keep costs down even more, they used what they called "efficient" (i.e., small) floor plans, stucco siding, tar and gravel roofs, and bulk orders of windows, decorative work, and hardware. Pragmatically, then, the character of these early stucco buildings derives from an even mix of fairly standardized parts. Ornament and fenestration are distributed across the surfaces of simple and compound boxes of conventional frame construction, with low sloped or flat roofs. But these houses were required to offer more than just economy; they "had to perpetuate the California image that helped entice the new factory workers to California instead of Montana or Texas."[4] Within these limits, but outside the bounds of a more formal approach to design, is an aesthetic repeated with observable consistency. Perhaps these people shared a basic desire, though usually unconscious and unspoken, to order and simplify the built environment and, because this was California, to revel in the landscape. Perhaps they perceived a new culture in which acceptance of the new did not seem to require rejection of the old. It would seem that the designer/builder, more readily than the trained professional, was able to allow this coexistence and felt free to choose among the numerous architectural styles available at the time.

The buildings come in so many shapes and sizes that their most identifiable characteristics, apart from the stucco cladding, are their use and height. The most common building, by far, is a single family house, either one-story (bungalow size) or two-story. Most of the rest are multiple unit dwellings, which tend as well to be one-story (duplexes) or two-story (four-plexes). The general character of the eclectic stucco building is its solid rectilinear massing, which is derived from the sculptural quality of stucco. The solid appearance of the stucco and the thickness of the architectural elements combine to evoke masonry construction.

The box rests squarely on the ground, with entry by way of broad stairs and a porch of monumental scale. The roof may be broad and hovering, borrowed from the Prairie School, or flat, with parapets, plain or articulated. Wood sash casements and Chicago windows, with glazing bars in Prairie School patterns, punctuate the facade. While planar modulations of the wall surface only suggest classical forms (pilasters, panels, corbels, etc.) or are simply abstract, the applied ornament is clearly of classical derivation. The horizontality of the Prairie School is employed, but the traditional disposition of architectural features precludes the dynamism of that style; a more Mediterranean character is the result. The mixed parentage of the eclectic stucco building is the key to its identity.

Although a number of examples can be found that adhere strictly to the canons of particular styles, most of the buildings, those that were constructed between 1910 and 1930, do not fit into any accepted categories; they constitute a style of their own. They are not so clearly defined that we can easily label them; but there are a number of identifiable sources, the relative importance of which can be examined.

In *Romantic California*, in the chapter titled "Italy in California," Ernest Peixotto states that "the choicer homes, too, affect the Latin type, and when not frankly Spanish, are built to recall the villas of Capri or Sorrento."[5] Clearly, one major response to the question of an architecture appropriate to California, with its Mediterranean climate and flower-filled gardens, was the importation of a style from that part of the Old World most closely resembling the Golden State.

Justification for this solution lay in the original settlement of California by Latins, many of whose ranchos and missions were still around, mostly in picturesquely compelling ruins. And from these piles of eroding adobe the Mission Revival style emerged in the last decade of the nineteenth century and became so popular that characteristics of the style began to appear in the late work of even the Newsom brothers, grand masters of the Queen Anne persuasion and authors of popular pattern books. At about the same time, the Pueblo (Indian) Revival enjoyed a more modest vogue. The buildings of both the Mission and

opposite, left
Stucco house, Long Beach, California, 1923
right
Stucco house, Oakland, California, 1916

left
Stucco house, Oakland, California, ca 1921
above
Stucco house, Oakland, California, 1926

Pueblo Revivals employed the aesthetic of adobe or stone, rough timber, and the primitive craftsmanship of their antecedents, though they abandoned characteristically tiny windows in favor of sunlight and views. California's luxuriant wilderness had been tamed and could now be enjoyed.

However, by the end of the first decade of the twentieth century, California's two indigenous persuasions, as well as the Craftsman style, had begun to be supplanted by the accurate reproduction of period styles, a number of academic revivals, and the growing influence of the Ecole des Beaux Arts in Paris. David Gebhard has said, "Architectural imagery has its inception at the top of the social ladder, and then slowly percolates down to the lower classes."[6] This suggests that as California's wealth and power grew, more of its citizens were turning to the high art buildings of Europe for inspiration. They, and gradually the burgeoning masses, began to think that California's pre-Yankee architecture was but a humble provincial version of the real thing. As the common man, prodded as he was from above, lost some of his excitement for the earlier indigenous styles, but still was not ready for high art, there was still a wide range of choices to turn to, full of new life and infinite adaptability and even a few recollections of a romantic classical past; and it was inexpensive. He grasped it wholeheartedly.

By the early part of the twentieth century, the Everyman architecture of the stucco building had begun to include certain references to the classical vocabulary of forms. Some of the sources were from Greece and Rome. It was found that the simple wood frame volumes, when stuccoed over, could resemble the plain massing of classical architecture. And sometimes the analogy was taken even further so that the cheap and pliable material allowed even a miniature temple facade to shade the front porch. More commonly though, for this was above all a practical architecture, the site and the floor plan determined the shape of the building, especially at the back, after the important first impression had been made. Classical decoration was also employed, some built on site, consisting of simple, rather abstract forms such as corbels, string courses, pilasters, panels, and arches. Manufactured classical ornament — pilasters, brackets, medallions, cartouches with acanthus scrolls and swags — was applied, either sparsely or profusely, with a certain eye for its appropriate location, though the builders sometimes placed it upside down. It is said that the Greeks made their first stone temples as replicas of earlier wooden ones. The stucco builders even reversed this tradition, starting off with a wooden building and then covering it with a plaster imitation of masonry. Still, except for a few trellises or ramadas or false beam ends, wood was rarely employed in a classical manner.

Most of the progressive trends that found a following in California came from or were filtered through Chicago by way of popular magazines.[7] The "Casement Window House" shown in *House Beautiful* in 1902 had English precedents in the work of Charles Voysey and Edwin Lutyens. The publication of Frank Lloyd Wright's "Fireproof House for $5,000" in a 1907 *Ladies Home Journal* had a large impact in the West. The work of the Viennese Secession was known through the *Craftsman Magazine*. Some fine renditions of Prairie School design were built in California, but of great-

above
**Stucco house,
Oakland, California,
1916**
right
**Stucco house,
Oakland, California,
1913**
far right
**Stucco house,
Long Beach, California,
1920**

were built in California, but of greater interest is the work of such sophisticated local designers as John Hudson Thomas or Irving Gill, who gleaned shapes and motifs from midwestern sources and began to use them in new ways. It gradually became possible, then, for speculative builders in California to observe firsthand buildings innovatively designed,[8] or at least to read about locally produced wonders in the magazines. The results were immediate. A builder in Piedmont,

California, for instance, actually copied Irving Gill's famous Lewis Courts after it had been published in the *Architect and Engineer.*[9]

Frank Lloyd Wright, in his Prairie School work, was credited with "breaking the box" by means of free-flowing floor plans and the placement of windows so that a wall would appear as a succession of planes rather than a single plane with holes in it. When it came to popularizing Wright's innovation, the California speculative builder revealed that he did not grasp the radical redefinition of space. For example, the versions of Prairie School houses reproduced in stucco never allowed windows to congregate at the corners where they might erode the box, but were positioned with an almost classical symmetry. Sometimes there were even quasi-pilasters at the corners to bind up the boxiness even further. The California builders struck a compromise between the Mediter-

ranean and the Progressive, between the weight and stability of the old, and the open and light, stucco on wood frame designs of the new. One of the major trade-offs was that the imitation of any style usually stopped at the front wall — the typical eclectic stucco building is a plain box with a fancy facade.

The use of numerous historical styles in these buildings seems to prefigure the more obvious characteristics of Post-Modernism, whose practitioners often combine studied versions of the past with pieces salvaged from the International Style. While the eclecticism of the stucco building stemmed from naivete, the results often resemble the outpourings of the post-modernist's "conscious schizophrenia."[11] The earlier buildings, however, are often bold, even in their crudeness, and convey a certain optimism. The work of the post-modernists is often tentative and mannered, even pedantic.

During the late nineteenth and early twentieth centuries, the imitators of historical styles and the proponents of progressive architecture had a lot in common. Though the progressive designers were working at being radical, they were still rooted, many by way of the Arts and Crafts movement, in human values; a building could be both humane and modern. The modern was not yet conceived as being cut off from the past. Le Corbusier's notion of a house as a "Machine for Living" would have been as disagreeable to Wright as to an historical allusionist. But the manifestos of modernism finally effected a rupture. "Modernist exclusivity and anti-historicism[12] brought about the ascendancy of an architecture of technological imagery, the International style, and it became increasingly difficult to be a member of both camps.

But even with the rise of modernism and the attendant decline of

left
Stucco house,
Long Beach, California,
1920
above
Typical two-story
stucco duplexes

|115

KIRK PETERSON

historical architecture, speculative builders in California continued to produce eclectic stucco buildings, from the early part of this century to the present. The vernacular of speculative stucco houses in particular has proved to be immune to the arguments of the Modern movement. So there has been a long and colorful parade of such enthusiasms: Hispanic/Streamline-Moderne hybrids; Ranch Style descendents of the Prairie School done up in lumpy stucco and red tile roofs; Popular Modern dingbat apartment buildings (with their aluminum slider variant of the "Chicago window"); and even Schindler's stucco and red tile Von Koerber house of 1931.

These eclectic buildings remain a major part of many of California's spread-out cities, where they lend "a certain charm which a more serious or dignified approach might not create."[13] Victorian houses, once anathema, are now precious,

once anathema, are now precious so these buildings may enjoy a similar change in status. Time has not yet ravaged this rich heritage, and the wheels of progress, except in Los Angeles, have managed to leave most of it intact. Some of the highest concentrations of eclectic stucco dwellings can be found in San Diego's Mission Hills community, in San Francisco's Richmond District, in north Berkeley, in Oakland's Lakeshore District, in Hollywood, and in Long Beach near the ocean, south of downtown.

Footnotes

1. Quoted in "Concrete Cottages in California," *Architect and Engineer,* vol. XXXI, January 1913, p.67.

2. Quoted by Lawrence Grow, *Outdoor Living Spaces,* New York: Main Street Press, 1981, p.24.

3. Robert Judson Clark, *California Design, 1910,* Pasadena: California Design Publications, 1974, p.135.

4. Paul Groth, *Ac 15: Oakland as a Cross Section of America's Urban Cultural Landscape*, Berkeley: University of California, 1980.

5. Ernest Peixotto, *Romantic California*, New York: Charles Scribner's Sons, 1911, p.4.

6. David Gebhard, in the foreword to Robert Winter's, *The Califoria Bungalow*, Los Angeles: Hennessey & Ingalls, 1980, p.7.

7. Some flow in the other direction did occur. Wright's Chauncey Williams House of 1895 includes a motif common in Mission Revival work: the Baroque window used on Carmel Mission.

8. Thomas Gordon Smith, "John Hudson Thomas and the Progressive Spirit of Architecture, 1910-1920," unpublished thesis (University of California, Berkeley, 1975), pp.56-57.

9. "Cottages," p.67.

10. Dr. G.C. Stockman House, Mason City, Iowa, 1908.

11. Helen Searing, *Speaking a New Classicism: American Architecture Now*, Northhampton, Mass.: Smith College Museum of Art, 1981, p.13.

12. Searing, *New Classicism*, p.16.

13. "Domestic Architecture that is Different," *Architect and Engineer*, February 1914, vol. XXXVI, p.48.

opposite
Typical two-story stucco houses
above
Typical one-story stucco houses

**John Beach and
John Chase**

THE
STUCCO
BOX

The stucco-surfaced speculative apartment house is the symbol, for good or ill, of one of the golden ages of Los Angeles, the 1950s. It was a time when Southern California seemed to come into its own as a place where social and economic mobility combined with the benign climate to create a mythic good life, accessible, it seemed, to almost everyone. The stucco box apartment house reflected at once the pragmatic and hedonistic character of Southern California. It was ruthlessly expedient, made out of the cheapest materials, by the simplest construction methods, shoehorning the maximum number of units possible onto its lot. At the same time, these buildings were glamorously packaged consumer objects that often permitted more contact with the outdoors, easier access to the auto, and greater recreational opportunities than had Los Angeles's earlier tenement style apartment houses.[1] Some stucco boxes were more daringly abstract and more completely modernistic than others; these are the buildings that we have chosen to focus on in this essay.

The stucco box apartment houses were generally two, or sometimes three-story wood frame, stucco-finished, 4-16 unit buildings constructed by small investors on single or paired 50-foot wide lots; though some had as many as 70 units, stretching far back from the street, built by contractor/owners or investment syndicates. Their interiors were functional and, if one discounted the decorative details such as the swag lamp or the occasional exotic finishes such as glitter-surfaced ceilings, rather minimal.

The stucco box was constructed as infill housing in already established neighborhoods, in the metropolitan core from Echo Park through Santa Monica and out to the San Fernando Valley, as well as in still developing suburban areas of Los Angeles, like Orange County

and the South Bay. It reached its fullest development as a type during the years from 1954, when it was spurred by the popularity of modernism, the Post World War II housing boom, and the mass-production of aluminum frame sliding windows, to the years 1957-60, when more rigorous parking requirements and changing tastes signaled its eventual demise.

The stucco box's basically neutral character as a building type, in contrast to the aggressively modernistic character of its ornament, set it apart from other apartment buildings.[2] In the stucco box, individual elements such as windows or roofs, which might have been separately articulated in a traditional architectural composition, were subsumed within the neutral envelope of the building. These elements were overlaid and often obscured by an abstract pattern of decoration.

The ornamental components of

the stucco box were normally confined to the publicly seen areas: to the street elevation, and, where there was one, to the courtyard. The sides and rear were treated in the most pragmatic and economical manner possible, resulting in large areas of smooth stucco wall, rhythmically repetitive window patterns, and cubic forms which sometimes hover over the voids of the carport. Windows were mass-produced, metal-frame units placed at the surface of the wall with no reveal, creating an image of a depthless plane, a light, technologically advanced membrane. The front of the stucco box was seldom austere (although there are exceptions), but from the side or rear most examples would seem quite comfortable if transported to one of the purist German housing exhibitions, even *Siedlungen* of the 1920s and '30s.

The concept of building a simple, box-like structure with the most easily available construction materials and methods and then fronting it with an elaborate facade was nothing new, especially in Los Angeles. Such box-like buildings had been used in residential buildings (among others) ever since the Spanish first settled the region. Turn-of-the-century brick or wood tenement buildings were often completely unadorned at their side and rear elevations. The chief difference between one of these earlier tenements and the stucco box was that the stucco box's materials lacked the sense of scale and three-dimensional depth of the brick or tongue-in-groove siding used earlier. Both brick and wood siding are composed of small elements and possess reveals between these elements that demonstrate their depth. Not only were the materials of the stucco box lacking in a sense of weight, plasticity, or physical presence, the manner in which they were treated made no attempt to hide this fact. The honesty of the stucco box was inadvertent, born of the ease with which the speculative developer could disguise economic necessity as modernistic chic.[3]

The stucco box designers developed a whole battery of highly original abstract effects that arose directly out of the nature of stucco as a medium. They scored it, in stripes and in grids, and painted it in contrasting colors. They scattered dark-colored sand or grit over light-colored walls to create a smoky overlay, and they imbedded small chips of pumice in the surface that gave it textural interest analogous to chocolate chip ice cream. Color was an integral part of the appeal of the stucco box, for much of its decoration was painted on rather than built. The colors themselves were often intense pastels, some of them never before used with such abandon in domestic architecture, often in drop-dead

combinations like black and pink or turquoise and gold.[4] In fact, the colors of the stucco box had more in common with the colors popular in automobile, fashion, advertising, industrial design, and Modern art in the 1950s than they had with previous residential building color palettes (with the possible exception of Victorian polychrome). Some of the lower-budget stucco boxes were so striped, their chief boast was that they did come in assorted colors,

like Easter eggs or Christmas tree balls.

The roof of the stucco box is often flat, though hipped or low-pitched roofs with the gable end facing the street were used where it was necessary to project a more conventional ideal of domesticity; butterfly roofs were sometimes incorporated to signify modernity.[5] Access to the apartments was most frequently provided in smaller buildings by a two-level exterior corri-

dor along one side, and in larger buildings by a central courtyard, wholly or partially surrounded by the open corridor. Ideally, the courtyard would contain a swimming pool, though more often it did not; but it was landscaped and paved to appear as a communal patio.

The lighting and landscaping of the stucco box were as exhibitionistic as the ornament. Plants were selected for the dramatic silhouettes, such as dracaena, sago palms, and agave, or for their luxuriant tropical foliage, such as philodendron and rubber plants. They were frequently isolated as sculptural elements or graphic accents. Exotic specimens, such as castor beans or a giant bird-of-paradise clump, might not be displayed as part of the landscape ensemble, but as an isolated abstract pattern, elaborately outlined and pierced against the even color field of the stucco surface. At night the wall

was further embroidered by intense shadows cast by carefully placed colored spotlights concealed in the front lawn or planting strip. The notion of completing a building with its landscape is reminiscent of the eighteenth century aesthetic of the Picturesque, but the manner in which this connection was accomplished is pure Hollywood.

The naming of the stucco box, as with its landscaping and lighting, was an integral part of its image and an important event for its owner. In the 1950s and '60s, Los Angeles rental property was an attractive investment for the reasonably well-off small investor. In many cases, the stucco box represented the life savings of its owner and was a solid, publicly displayed symbol of personal success. Pride in this accomplishment accounts for the frequency with which stucco boxes were given human names, just as a boat might: The *Melody*

Ann, for instance, in Inglewood, or last names such as *Muscat Apartments* in Echo Park. Sometimes the name evokes other places and other times, both future and past: *Telstar* in the San Fernando Valley, or the *Algiers* in Rosemead. Often the name might refer to the location of the building, such as the *Cinema* in Hollywood, or be a pun on a street name, as in the *Rocks of Gibraltar* on Gibraltar Street in Baldwin Hills or the *Fountain Blu* on

Fountain Avenue. The *Beverly Wilton*, standing at the intersection of Beverly and Wilton, seems wistfully to aspire to Beverly Hiltonhood. Many of the names had escapist connotations of resort hotels or Las Vegas casinos — the *Sands, Palms, Dunes,* and *Capri.* Not surprisingly, in a place and time when pride in suburban yards was such an important social phenomenon, some stucco box names included the word garden. The

names are so important because these buildings are packaged objects, and the name is the label on that object.

The Los Angeles architect, Jack Chernoff, who has designed some 2,000 apartment buildings to date, many of them stucco boxes, is probably as good a person as any to illustrate the methods of a stucco box designer. Chernoff's typical client for a stucco box apartment was "a guy in the needle trade,

maybe a small manufacturer, who pulled together 10, 15, 20 thousand dollars to buy a lot."[6] Many of these buildings had an approximately equal number of 650-700 square-foot one-bedroom units and 900 square-foot two-bedroom units. "Hopefully it [the apartment building] would make the investor a living, but it would not make him rich," Chernoff noted. At some points in the Post World War II housing market there was an oversupply of units, and apartment owners were forced to offer two or three months free rent to their prospective tenants. Many of Chernoff's clients lived in the rear units of their four to six unit buildings, some of them for twenty years or more.

Using a set cost of eight to ten dollars a square foot, Chernoff would attempt to "pack" the building as full of units as the parking requirements would allow by eliminating hallway space and by open-

ing up the kitchen to the living-dining room.[7] Speaking of some apartments he had then recently designed, Chernoff was quoted in a 1972 *Los Angeles Times:* "We're looking for some dramatic punch that'll bring tenants in. Most important is an attractive exterior. We give them enough to get them in, not more. We don't waste any money on exteriors. Once they're in, they have to love these apartments...We give them the illusion of

space. We'll cram in as many units as we can. I ask myself what can I cram in here and still get a nice feeling?"[8] Chernoff went on to state that the buildings had flat facades and flat roofs because the two went together well and because they were the most economical choices possible.

The stucco box was well suited to the newcomer in Los Angeles, a city with numerous immigrants and a great need for temporary homes.

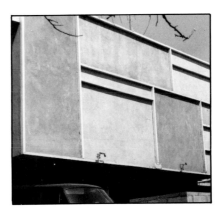

During the stucco box era, there was no shortage of newcomers to the Los Angeles area: its population increased by two million each decade during the 1940s and '50s, tapering off to only a million in the 1960s. Apartment construction reflected this trend: large numbers of them were built in the period from 1952 to 1966.[9]

The stucco box inhabitant was often single or newly married, and upwardly mobile. He or she might not have considered the apartment as a permanent way of life, as may have been the case in denser American cities. So the stucco box maintained some of the social amenities of the bungalow court, a type initially developed, in part, as carefree vacation accommodation. These apartments were viewed, not simply as a place of temporary shelter, but as an introduction to the near-mythic, and much written about, social, sexual, and climatic conditions of California living.

The automobile was an important influence on the stucco box. It literally became part of the building, on display in the carport. The need to accommodate it helped to determine the form of the building and how much area would be left available, or rendered unavailable, for landscaping. Parking was most frequently provided at grade level, on the periphery of the building, as an open carport that was recessed along one or more of its sides. If parking was required along the street facade, the second floor would often float on thin pipes above the void of the carport to become a light technological object separate from the landscape in characteristic high-art modernist fashion. In some cases this arrangement took on the uncanny aspect of pop homage to Le Corbusier's villas of the 1920s and '30s, particularly when strip windows were joined together with a molding surround.[10]

garage fitted easily into both the aesthetic of the post-war, post-and-beam school of high-art Southern California modernism and the aesthetic of the developer's stucco box apartment. Speculative builders may, in fact, have been a step or two ahead of the high-art architects in their use of open carports, though several carport projects by the latter were published in *Arts and Architecture* magazine during the first half of the 1950s.[11]

Placing the garage at the front of a residential building was nothing new in Los Angeles — it had become commonplace in projects by modernist architects such as the Laurelwood apartments of 1948 by R.M. Schindler or the Strathmore apartments of 1937 by Richard Neutra. Still, however much their garage or carports were on display, the automobile itself was invariably hidden behind screens or garage walls and doors. It was not until after World War II that architects and speculative builders began taking the doors, and sometimes the side walls, off garages so that the automobile and the negative form of the garage space became part of the design.

The advantages of this approach were several: it was economical, it eliminated the maintenance of garage doors, and it made it easier to get the auto in and out of its parking space. Stylistically, the airiness and insubstantiality of the open

Parking was the chief limit on the size of stucco box development. According to the ratio of floor area to building lot area permitted by the zoning code, most stucco boxes could have held more units than they actually did; but it was often impossible to provide the parking spaces necessary to build up to this limit. Doing so would often have meant the inclusion of a concrete subterranean parking garage and a possible third or fourth story at greater expense. This type of larger apartment house with three or more stories over sunken parking became more common in the 1960s, because of intensified development pressures and changes in parking requirements. After World War II, parking requirements had generally held at an even level until 1957, when additional spaces were required per unit. In 1969 the requirement was upped again.[12] Another change in parking laws during the 1960s outlawed a favorite stucco box device, back-out parking, which had borrowed the front-yard setback, the sidewalk, and the street for use as the access lane of a conventional parking lot or garage.

As important as parking in determining the look of the stucco box were its surface materials: the stucco finish of its walls, the ornament and trim added to these walls, and the aluminum-frame sliding windows. In the United States, the

introduction of metal frame sliding windows was closely linked to the introduction of custom sliding glass doors, which began to appear just before World War II. The early doors were first made of steel, later of wood and steel, then wood and aluminum, and finally, all aluminum.[13] Sliding windows had been made of steel in the late '40s and early '50s, but they frequently jammed. The steel sliders were replaced by aluminum sliders, in part, because the use of aluminum in the war effort had helped to lower its cost. Alcoa manufactured aluminum double-hung windows as early as 1950.[14] By 1954 the use of mass-produced, aluminum-frame sliding windows and standard sizes (6' x 6'8") for sliding doors became widespread. In effect the window was pushed almost flush with the wall plane, emphasizing the overall appearance of paper thinness. Another common aluminum frame window treatment of approximately

the same era was a large pane of fixed-glass flanked by panels of louvered jalousies.

Stucco as a material, regardless of its particular application has had a very bad press. The stucco box is no exception to this. The "whited sepulchere," the Biblical metaphor for the suave surface concealing unspecified corruption, is perhaps the earliest slur. And today there is the illogical but apparently ineradicable attitude that since stucco is

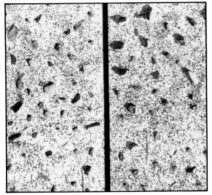

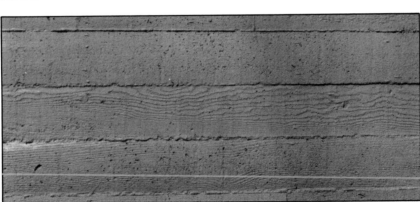

purely a surface material, what it covers must be unhealthy or immoral. Perhaps the ease with which stucco can be used to fake other materials such as marble, brick, and even wood bark, is responsible for the general suspicion of critics and historians, particularly those of twentieth century purist persuasion. Still, the versatility and economy of stucco have made it a valuable material for vernacular builders and for many high-art

designers in Southern California, including Wright, Schindler, Ain, and Neutra, among others.[15] By the 1920s, California was a stuccic Eden; its stucco surfaces had evolved into a defined vernacular wood-framed construction type with a standard set of techniques, details, and costs for its finishes. It was the thinness of stucco's chicken-wire and building paper base, placed over wood studs 16" on center, that made it possible for the stucco box to appear so sharp-edged.

The style that this pragmatically determined building type was arrayed in was that of modernism, popularly adapted from the world of high-art architecture. A high-art style that ventures into the vernacular world must have a series of trademarks that can be immediately grasped by those with no architectural training or knowledge. These trademarks are not mere stylistic gestures: they have

become metaphors for a wide range of aesthetic, psychological, and historical associations; in short, a complete set of attitudes about life and art. In the case of modernism, these peripheral but indispensable associations include abstract art, the stream of consciousness novel, Freud, plastic, speed, cinema, and technological progress. This same set of associations has been evoked at successive stages by periodically updated

sets of images and details.

The trademarks of vernacular modernism in the 1950s and '60s were taken from four primary sources: high-art architecture, abstract art, automobile design, and interior decoration. It is no coincidence that the most ebulliently modernistic apartment houses were built during the 1950s, while Detroit was turning out the most flamboyantly modernistic automobiles in history. The moxie of 1950s

auto design, in such details as two-tone paint jobs or harlequin patterns on the dashboards, set a level of sophistication and daring for other artifacts of that decade to equal, even as the auto stylists themselves were influenced by the prevailing fashions of the times. Both the tail-fin on the automobile and the starburst light on the stucco box were indications that the consumer products they were attached to were new, exciting, and up-to-date.

Borrowing from the local tradition of high-art architectural modernism, apartment builders converted the exhibitionistic expression of John Lautner and Lloyd Wright into a graphic language of pattern and decoration. One commonly used motif was a bas-relief or semi-detached rectangular plane, often surfaced with fieldstone or a scored grid pattern. It had formal precedents in the constructivist tendencies of local work by Schind-

ler and Neutra and a number of others.[16]

A major influence on all popular design of the 1950s and one much loved by the builders of the stucco box was the abstraction at that time in high-art painting and sculpture. Starkly counterpoised rectangles, versions of the ones by Mondrian, were likely to appear in the design of clocks, jewelry, ceramics, magazine layouts, and stucco box facades. Less popular, although

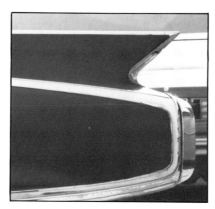

building, but they were almost never used to shape the structure itself; unless distorted by environmental circumstance, the stucco box remained rigidly orthogonal because of traditional economies of construction.[18]

Although the entire facade was frequently treated as an environmentally-scaled abstract relief, it was also common practice to treat the elevation as an interior wall, in the manner of an interior decorator,

with objects placed upon it just as one might find in a contemporary living room. The swag lamp, the wall sconce, the picture frame, the ornamental plaque, and the shadow box were all devices of interior decoration that were placed on the street facade as if to symbolize the quasi-public nature of the life that was led there.[19] The shared courtyard and the walkways that functioned as balconies, with or without their swimming pool, served in the

still common, were the boomerang and kidney shapes of coffee tables and ashtrays also to be found on fabrics and Formica.[17] Counterpoised rectangles and boomerangs appear in the stucco box primarily as two-dimensional cutouts mounted flat on the wall plane, but they also occur in plan as entrance canopies, planters, and swimming pools. These carefully irregular forms were freely employed to enrich the appearance of the

the apartment house. Usually the tone was modernist, though some of its parts clearly aspired to the Baroque, particularly in the light fixtures and wall coverings.

The abstraction and minimalism inherent in the stucco box, combined with its inherently utilitarian bent, produced some facades that were simply blank walls, interrupted only by the entrance, the address, two or three lights, and perhaps a few bits of scattered ornament. By the 1950s in Los Angeles the need for privacy was often more important than any desire to maintain contact with the street. The cheapness and the modernistic cachet of these dazzlingly blank facades allowed the stucco box designers to ignore orthodox notions of welcoming domesticity that the inclusion of windows on a facade might have conveyed.

In Southern California the modernism of the stucco box was part of a regional vernacular. Despite the fact that we are frequently informed nowadays that modernism was never popular, the phenomenal sales figures for free-form ashtrays, Finnish dinnerware, and wire-basket chairs during the 1950s and early '60s prove otherwise. Expressionistic modernism had the power to engage the popular imagination because it could serve as a vehicle for personal fantasy. It dominated commercial vernacular

architecture in Southern California for more than a decade.

From the late 1950s until the mid-1960s modernist high-art buildings were publicized in Southern California newspapers as well as in the professional magazines. Almost every issue of the *Home* section of the Sunday *Los Angeles Times* would feature at least one modernist residence, which might have also appeared in the banner carrier for Southern California

literature of the period, and not infrequently in actuality, as outdoor rooms for parties, barbeques, and general socializing.

One variant of the stucco box building type, used either to indicate an especially high level of poshness and/or to accommodate an elevator, featured a vestibule in which the street wall was almost completely glazed. This glazing created a space not unlike the one-wall-removed convention of traditional set design. Inside were the real icons of interior decoration, carefully chosen and arranged for public view: elaborate flocked wallpaper, an ornamental plaque large enough to be seen from the street, a chandelier or swagged hanging lamp — overscaled and of complex design — and at least one indoor plant capable of casting dramatic shadows. This entry-cum-showcase, distributed its eclat equally among the inhabitants of modernism, the magazine *Arts and Architecture*, available at many local newsstands alongside *Time* and *The New Yorker*.[20]

These published buildings were studied, interpreted, and reinterpreted by clients, developers, and builders who probably owned a component hi-fi system, a slat-bench coffee table, and a reasonably late model automobile. Some of these partisans of the modern felt that historical reference in their personal environment was at best dishonest and at worst unsophisticated. They formed a public that was highly self-conscious of living in the twentieth century and they demanded an up-to-date backdrop for their everyday life. It was not a rigorous, theoretical, or high-art modernism that they wanted; rather, it was accommodating, inexpensive, and vernacular.

However, the commitment of the owner and designers of the stucco box to modernism was often more superficial or fashionable than it was heart-felt. The stucco box did have to accommodate itself to a certain range of lot configurations, changes in grade, and varied budgets, but its organization and layout was determined according to set formulas. The aesthetic decisions that could fit into these formulas were largely those of packaging. While the decoration of the stucco box often celebrated modernism, there was less enthusiasm for the vitality of its architectural vocabulary than there was for its cheapness. The grilles, frames, and panels that were applied to the stucco box could even be made out of scrap wood. It was possible to use such ephemeral effects on the stucco box because its decoration was flat and graphic. The inexpensive materials worked well because the aesthetic of the stucco box did not demand that they appear to be anything other than additive, decorative, abstract pat-

terns in which the pattern was much more important than the material it was made from.

Infrequently, the basically modernist stucco box was overlaid with period revival elements, usually exotic ones, ranging from Aztec to Assyrian. But the designers did not attempt to create a complete period revival environment of another time or place as was the fashion in the 1920s or '30s. Rather, they would place a few signifying

fragments of the style in question at some crucial focus, normally the entrance, in an otherwise modernist facade, just as an archeological artifact might be displayed on a pedestal in a white-painted room of a museum.

The neutral box could also accommodate decoration that symbolized other themes. In the 1950s the imagery of the "Modern Colonial" and the suburban Ranch style house, with its mock hand-hewn siding and diamond paned windows, was a distant runner-up in popularity to modernistic themes for smaller apartment houses in Southern California. The 1960s ushered in a period of renewed stylistic eclecticism, rivaling that of the 1920s and '30s in California in the breadth, although not the depth, of its references. Polynesian and Oriental motifs were popular during the early 1960s. Motifs adapted from the Hollywood Regency style, such as false-fronted mansards and vertically exaggerated, arched Pullman doors, were widespread. The mansard theme, which has proved extremely durable in Los Angeles, has passed into the general vocabulary of the area's popular architecture, combining with and symbolizing a variety of styles.[21]

As an example of rapid changes in fashion, the stucco box is representative of the commercial vernacular. While high-art architecture influenced the remodels and, to a certain extent, legitimized the ruthless utilitarianism of stripped side and rear walls, the stucco boxes were chiefly influenced by each other. Some vernacular modes of building have evolved over a long period of time, but the vernacular of the stucco box was couched in the quickly changing, media-popularized styles of a consumer society.

As the Post World War II era perplexingly and obstinately refused to resolve into a technological utopia, and as concern about the toxic side effect of technological processes spread, modernism began to slip down the architectural Top 40.[22] Changed attitudes towards technology have had an effect upon the form as well as the imagery of the speculative apartment block. As the price of fossil fuel goes up, so does the value of older, close-in Los Angeles neighborhoods. Earlier buildings, and

art architecture as Frank Lloyd Wright's late work, much less such vernacular accomplishments as the stucco box. The stucco box, then, has been consistently attacked because it was not modern, and because it was. And it has become an easy mark for satirists because it has been fashionable to make light of Los Angeles, and consequently to make light of one of its most provocative symbols, the stucco box.

In fact, the stucco box was mod-

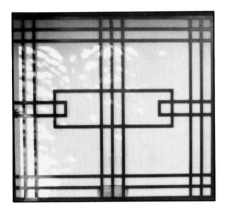

even entire neighborhoods, have been bulldozed for new multiple-unit speculative buildings that are larger and denser than the stucco box, just as the stucco box itself had often replaced earlier single-family houses. The generally larger buildings of the 1960s created problems of scale and density, although it could be argued that stylistic invention continued to be as lively as ever.

Los Angeles's popular modernist stucco box has become an artifact, representative of relatively stable social values, faith in technological process, and an endless upward mobility. Current post-modernist sensibility, while sympathetic to most vernacular phenomena, rejects associations with modernism, because it considers modernism passe. At the same time, modernism has been defined by many critics in such a way as to avoid the serious evaluation of such non-purist variants of orthodox high-

ernist in its image and, to a degree, in its matter-of-fact acceptance of the most readily available technology. In vernacular fashion, it grafted the new upon the old to create a product that was simultaneously forward-looking and comfortably familiar. Also, its ability to symbolize Los Angeles and to symbolize modernism, in the mind of the critic and in the mind of the vernacular builder and his client, points out the importance of the stucco box as a case study in vernacular architecture from the recent past.[23] The stucco box provided a living environment that was a clean well-lighted space, at a human scale, for a reasonable price, and with the popular approval to which high-art modernism aspired, but too seldom achieved.

Footnotes

1. It is difficult to know whether to classify the stucco box as a 1940s garden apartment denuded of much of

its garden or as a miniature tenement that has gained a garnish of landscaping. The imagery is that of the resort, redolent with an air of escapism which might ingenuously refer to the tropics, as readily as to an outer space journey. This notion of being on vacation all year round was symbolized by the landscaping, the lighting, the graphics, and the outdoor access to all the units. The lack of overhanging eaves and the brilliant expanses of wall made them seem to reflect the glare of the California sun-

shine with redoubled intensity. For this reason the stucco box is a descendant of courtyard housing, even though many of them had nary a courtyard, or even a real sideyard to call their own, and often equalled or surpassed the high ratio of lot coverage achieved by the tenements of the 1895-1930 era in Los Angeles. On courtyard housing see Laura Chase's article on bungalow courts, "Eden in the Orange Groves," *Landscape Magazine*, 1981, vol. 25, pp.29-36, and Stefanos Polyzoides,

Roger Sherwood, and James Tice, *Courtyard Housing in Los Angeles,* Berkeley: University of California Press, 1982.

2. Nor was there anything precedent-setting about the use of overtly modern imagery for speculative apartment houses in Los Angeles. The Streamline Moderne of the 1930s used rounded corners, pipe railings, and flat roofs to suggest the excitement of the machine age. The use of modern imagery, albeit of a different order, became even more common in the post-war 1940s.

3. Prior to the stucco box, stucco had been used far more often to simulate thick masonry walls, as in the Spanish Colonial Revival, than it had been used to express its actual paper-thin thickness. Local precedents for the stucco box include such examples as Lloyd Wright's 1926 Sowden house, in which fragments of elaborate ornamentation are added to the exterior of an otherwise ruthlessly plain stucco box. See John Beach, "Lloyd Wright's Sowden House, Bizarre Shapes from Custom-Cast Concrete Blocks," *Fine Home Building,* April-May 1983, pp.66-73.

4. In more suburban settings, such as sections of the San Gabriel or San Fernando Valleys, the vocabulary of the 1950s stucco box and, especially its site planning, might more closely resemble that of the 1940s garden apartment.

5. When pitched roofs were employed, they were often exaggerated and stretched to great lengths, with the gable and the body of the building expressed as a single volumetric whole. When the butterfly roof was employed, it was often terminated by a flat horizontal sunshade/entablature, which appeared as though the thin roof plane had simply been folded downward at the right angle. Frequently found in modernistic coffee shop buildings contemporaneous with the stucco box, it was a roof form borrowed from the expressionistic modernism of Frank Lloyd Wright (Taliesin West, 1938-59), John

Lautner (Googie's Coffee Shop, 1947), R.M. Schindler (Van Dekker house, 1940; Rodriguez house, 1941), and Richard Neutra (Nesbitt house, 1942).

6. Interview with Jack Chernoff by John Chase, March, 1983.

7. The idea of the combined living and dining room open to the kitchen (aside from one-room efficiency apartments) was not adopted until the 1940s in Southern California and did not become widespread until the 1950s. An early example is Sumner Spaulding and John Rex, architects, "Apartments for Nurses," in *Arts and Architecture,* October 1948, p.30.

8. Bob Nero, "The Blooming of the Plastic Apartment House," *Los Angeles Times West* magazine, February 13, 1972, pp.24-31.

9. Apartment building permits in the city of Los Angeles remained at approximately 1100-1600 per year, beginning in 1952, until the peak years of 1963 and 1964, when there were 2300 permits issued per year. The number of permits slid back down to 1600 in 1965 and then collapsed in 1966 to 300. It was not until 1975 that the number of permits began to increase again. Statistics obtained from the Building Department, City of Los Angeles.

10. The window facing exaggerated to appear as a frame was a legacy of the 1940s. In the 1950s it was extended to include more than one window, creating an ambiguity of scale which sometimes overlapped the visual effect of the ribbon window/grille. One does not see the windows; the grille reads as an abstract scaleless stripe or band. The ribbon window is thus transformed into an ornamental device.

11. Some relevant citations from *Arts and Architecture* are "Hillside Apartments," Campbell & Wong, May 1951, pp.32-33; "Hillside House," by Carl Louis Maston, November 1952, pp.32-33; "Small Apartment by Raymond Kappe, Architect," January 1955, p.27; "House by Craig Ellwood," October 1952, p.30; "Rental Housing designed by Greta

Magnusson Grossman," May 1952, p.32; "Small Apartments by Carl Louis Maston, architect," September 1952, p.24; "Six-Unit Apartment," Carl Louis Maston, architect, February 1952, p.27; and "Apartment Building" by Gregory Ain, April 1965, pp.20-21.

12. From 1948 to 1958, parking space per unit was mandated for a unit of more than three habitable rooms. In 1958 the parking ordinance was stiffened to a ratio of 1.25 spaces per each 3+ room unit and to one space per each 3 room unit. It was further tightened in 1968 when the ratio was upped to 2 spaces per each 3+ room unit and 1.5 spaces per each 3 room unit. Compiled from the Los Angeles Planning and Zoning codes.

13. The early sliding doors were hung from the bottom of their frame and often jammed. Carl Dumbolton, an architect, designed an improved bottom-rolling door for the Arcadia Metal Products Company. (Interview with Rudy Hodal of Carmel Metal Products by Laural Weintraub, November, 1982.) Advertisements for steel-frame metal sliding doors by the Glide and Steelbilt Companies first appeared in *Arts and Architecture* magazine in 1948.

14. The first advertisement for mass produced aluminum frame sliding windows and doors ran in *Arts and Architecture* in January, 1954, for Ador, followed shortly by the Miller, Panavision, Glide, and Slideview product lines.

15. In California, the use of stucco was first revived as one of the many finishes employed in Queen Anne buildings of the 1880s, principally in small panels in the gables of houses. Buildings partially or entirely sheathed in stucco did not begin to appear regularly until the 1890s as part of the Mission Revival style, when stucco was used on wood frame buildings to suggest adobe construction. The plainness of its surfaces also lent it more general Craftsman associations, as found, for example, in some of Irving Gill's earlier buildings.

16. This planar fragmentation is visible in some of Richard Neutra's work, especially the Kaufmann house of 1946, where a somewhat constructivist, de Stijl attitude to the International style is emphasized, contrasting stone with stucco walls. The visual and spatial explosion of the box was further popularized in the early 1950s work of Carl Maston, Ray Kappe, Thornton Ladd, and Greta Magnusson Grossman.

17. George Nelson's splashy starburst clock models may have served as a precedent for the innumerable starburst lights on the front facades of the stucco box. Typically, these shallow bowl-shaped lamps were mounted nearly flush to the wall surface and lit from behind. Often pierced with tiny holes, they exploded outward in a halo of long spikes. Nelson's clocks were first advertised in 1951 in *Arts and Architecture.*

18. However, it must be noted that it was precisely because of this customary orthogonal conformity that the infrequent

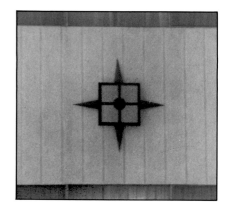

exceptions are often the most appealing. It is because these exceptions have plastic as well as graphic interest. Occasionally a change in grade might cause the ceiling of a carport to be sloped rather than flat, or very rarely the edge of the building above the carport might be chamfered. In some cases the stucco boxes were given fins or appendages that made them appear to be sculpturally configured. Apartments built on triangular lots or in spaces left over by freeway construction were frequently given added character by the speculative builders' straightforward accommodations to these circumstances.

19. For a discussion of the techniques and attitudes of the interior decorator as an architectural designer see John Chase, *Exterior Decoration: Hollywood's Inside-Out Houses*, Los Angeles: Hennessey & Ingalls, 1982.

20. Another publication that was a possible source for stucco box designers was the magazine *House and Home.* Some of its articles relevant to this study include one on expressionistic popular modernism, "Googie Architecture," February 1952, pp.86-88; followed in the same issue by a description of John Lautner's work, pp.89-91, and preceded by Raphael Soriano's Colby apartments, pp.67-73. Also in *House and Home* were Kenneth N. Lind's Sunset Apartments in Pacific Palisades, April 1952, p.101; Elliot Noyes's house at New Canaan, Connecticut, January 1953,

pp.118-121; and "Frank Lloyd Wright and 1,000,000 Houses a Year," March 1953, pp.105-09.

21. When first widely employed in Southern California, at the end of the 1950s, the mansard signified simply by its presence, two specific, totally opposed tendencies. The traditionalists could identify with French elegance. The modernists could relate its heavily simplified form to the sloped forms found in Frank Lloyd Wright's work of the late 1930s and '40s, such as Taliesin West, the Pauson house, and the Auldbrass Plantation.

22. For a discussion of historicism and expressionism in the context of Modern American architecture in the 1950s, see Suzanne Stephens, "Precursors of Post Modernism," *American Architecture After Modernism,* Robert Stern, ed., *A + U* Extra Edition, March 1981, pp.305-335. The two principal books concerned with post World War II modernism in Southern California are: Esther McCoy, *Case Study Houses,* Los

Angeles: Hennessey & Ingalls, 1977 and Herbert Weisskamp, *Beautiful Homes and Gardens in California,* New York: Harry N. Abrams Inc., 1964.

23. The bibliography of the stucco box is brief. David Gebhard discusses the role of the neutral stucco building in Southern California in "L.A., the Stucco Box," *Art in America* 58, May-June 1970, pp.130-133. The earliest publication of commercial vernacular post

World War II houses were Ed Ruscha, *Some Los Angeles Apartments,* Los Angeles: published by the author, 1965, which presents dead-pan pop-art snapshots with no other information given than the apartments' addresses. Reyner Banham offers up the stucco box under the cheerful pejorative term "dingbat architecture" in *Los Angeles: the Architecture of Four Ecologies,* Harmondsworth, England: Pelican Books, 1973, pp.175-77, 185. Charles Jencks,

Daydream Houses of Los Angeles, New York: Rizzoli, 1978 has a stucco box pictured on page 52 and a 1960s post-stucco box on the following page. The text of the book attempts to make Southern California out to be the flipped-out polyvinylchloride Shangri-la that so many English architects and critics want Los Angeles to be. An initial definition of the stucco box apartment house as a type may be found in Chase, *Exterior Decoration,* 66.

opposite
Sheet music for Dream
House, *P.M. Griffith, 1928*
above
Set still
right
Cartoon still, Clown of
the Jungle, *©1946, Walt
Disney Productions*

*We have taken it, as these shows developed together, that Home
Sweet Home, "vernacular" as it may be for a vast egalitarian nation, is not likely to be altogether anonymous, entirely separate
from individual taste and fancy. We share, I suppose, cautious ad-
miration for what Jorge Luis Borges described as "the democratic
superstition that postulates reserved merit for any anonymous
work, as though we all knew as a group what no single person
knows, as though intelligence were nervous and performed better
when no one was watching." But, on the other hand, we came
from a variety of places by a variety of routes, and many of the
dreams we dream about the buildings we build are individual,
even unique, not anonymous at all. "The Temple, the Cabin, and
the Trailer" show looks for the continuing oppositions conjoined
that animate our building: the spiritual in the practical, the cabin
in the temple (and the temple in the cabin), the simultaneous plain
and fancy, the private in the public, and the public in the private.
And it notes how much cultural baggage we carry along, mobile
as we are, and how fully we are drenched in dreams, individual
as well as shared.*
—P.B.

AND
DRENCHED
IN
DREAMS

Charles W. Moore

THE TEMPLE, THE CABIN, AND THE TRAILER

Other dramatizations of the vernacular have reveled in what Frank Lloyd Wright used to call the autochthonous, the work of people tied to the land, with emphasis on the simple, sculpturally dazzling, white-walled villages of Mediterranean places, the Greek islands in particular. While these dramatizations reveled in the autochthonous, they reviled the pretentious or even the learned, the importation of images from somewhere beyond that stretch of land, of the exotic, and of the fancy. They gloried, you might say, in the roots of this vernacular plant and cast dark aspersions on the branches and, especially, on the flowers. The present exhibition, on the contrary, sees the same vernacular energies in the commonplace as in the special, the one-off, the individual, the exotic, even the eccentric. We have taken our theme from the log, the straight trunk of the tree, perhaps even with the bark left on or perhaps hewn into a rough square in section. In a few of our Middle Atlantic beginnings and then in a substantial part of the forested interior of our continent, cabins were built up with horizontal logs which were notched and interlocked at the corners; the resulting pen, or room, roofed and sometimes multiplied, got built into the log cabin, which, after a couple of political campaigns, became a special symbol of American demo-

above
First house built in Utah, Salt Lake City, Utah, 1847
right
Fort Parker, near Groesbeck, Texas
far right
Log cabin with sod roof

cratic vernacular. The exhibition describes a few log cabins, their limitations as well as their political glory.

But then those same logs that provided shelter and little more except as a symbol of democratic virutes can be turned up on end. Here is where our story gets more intense. The top end can be decorated in ways academic or dreamlike. A roof can be placed over a porch of two or more of these upended logs, suitably decorated, and then we have, presto, a temple, a symbol, some say, of the upright position of the human body, unique among creatures of this planet (except maybe the penguin); it is certainly a visualization of the vertical axis, the axis mundi, the connection between earth and heaven, between humankind's base nature and our spiritual aspirations.

The exhibition goes on to consider a number of united opposites, beyond the horizontal and the ver-

tical of cabin and temple: it looks at the academic, the orthodox, on the one hand, and the ad hoc, the special, even the eccentric, on the other. It takes some of the vertical logs and gives them at first no decoration at the top, then stocking caps of the classical orders, the Doric, Ionic, Corinthian, and Composite that meant so much to generations of Americans, commonfolk as well as aristocrats, during the decades after our political independence. The eccentric we show, as well, our version of what Americans tried to invent from orders make of our native corn and tobacco to butterflies and kites.

A special thing about Americans, of course, is that we are not, by in large, peasants, not attached to the piece of land that our ancestors have farmed and dominated for generations. Although that still happens occasionally. Almost all of us are new-comers in the place where we are, wanderers bringing what

far left
**Mission Church,
northern Idaho**
left
**Roman Forum,
Rome, Italy**
above, top
**Dr. Wood's house,
Mokelumne Hill,
California, 1853**
above, bottom
**Houses, L.B.J. Ranch,
Johnson City, Texas**

used to be called a Yankee ingenious responsiveness to our dealings with a new place; but we also bring dreams and maybe even homesick fantasies about someplace far away from which we've come or someplace far away in both time and space about which perhaps we've read (some generations of Americans have been far more bookish than others). A special and very beautiful case in point is the house in Marshall, Michigan, built a hundred years ago by the U.S. consul of the Sandwich Islands (now Hawaii) on his return from his exotic tour of duty, a splendid intermingling of near and far visions of what was around him with dreams of places far away in time and space.

The vernacular comprises in our version the plain of the log cabin and the fancy, perhaps literary or perhaps formal, the elaborate and the playful. Shaker buildings and

furniture continue the log cabin's humble tradition of plain, and the members of gingerbreaded houses elaborate across the country, cheaply and inexpensively, our desire for putting on the dog.

Our dreams transport us at once into the realm of the big and the small. Our candidate for all the qualities we have been describing, writ large, is the Old Faithful Lodge in Yellowstone National Park, the apotheosis of the log cabin. An interesting candidate for the small are the Sunday houses of Fredericksburg, Texas, tiny houses built as part of the real estate conception that brought settlers from Germany to the hill country of central Texas; they were vacation houses turned inside out, built along the streets of the town so that people who lived on far-off ranches could go shopping on Saturday and attend church on Sunday.

The buildings of our American

vernacular are sometimes short and sometimes tall. The tall ones include not only the single-family house but also, from time to time in our past, the houses of God with their spires and the courthouses with their sometimes magnificent pinnacles reaching up that axis mundi toward heaven. Among other houses of God we show is the church built by the Czech community at Prague, Texas, a single simple spire pointing to the sky and almost reaching it. We look at the Ellis County Courthouse in Waxahachie, Texas, one of a number of extraordinary Texas courthouses of the 1890s, built fancy and big and tall with the energies and aspirations of the whole county. And we examine a house of entertainment in Merced, California, the Merced Theater, which is also tower. We have, too, the towered city hall of Beverly Hills, California, with its imagery fashioned more completely out of the dreams of an exotic Mediterranean place, mixed-up, to be sure, with the practicalities and enthusiasms of the here and now.

We deal with the permanent and temporary, as well, with some inversion of eternity, or at least of a long period of human inhabitation on this planet, demonstrated on the one hand, in the academic orders and in their vernacular Georgian descendants (the "Colonial" house has by now been with us for a very long time). On the other hand, the power of the new, the fashionable, the trendy, has always been strong in America, though perhaps never stronger than it is now when so many messages come at Americans from the little box and from every side.

Then, there is dramatic content in the fixed and the moveable, in the attempt, on the one hand, to set up permanent places on the frontier or in the wilderness, and the attempt, on the other hand, for so many of us to maintain our freedom to move, which shows up in dwellings that move, houseboats and trailers, as were described much earlier on in this catalog. Our exhibition includes, in addition ot trailers that move or once moved, such portable phenomena as the Cady House in the California mother Lode, built with pieces, some of them pretty fancy, that came around the Horn and were assembled into permanent dwellings. We also have a look at the amazing chapter in American domestic vernacular building when Sears and Roebuck maintained a catalog of pieces of remarkable elaborate houses which people could and did put together on their sites across the country.

What this exhibition really deals with is cultural baggage, the imperatives as well as the enthusiasms that we Americans have brought with us from somewhere else. We have combined this baggage with our responses to a particular landscape, setting, neighbors, and set a climatic and other conditions. We could have packed all of it into a set of suitcases and duffle bags and steamer trunks and cosmetic cases, but instead we found ourselves arranging our examples into what could be called vernacular commandments: thou shalt make it shelter, habitable, fit, and neat; but, not content with that, thou shalt make it look like something and then invest it with dreams, perhaps miniaturizing or enlarging it, perhaps sending it toward heaven, or perhaps making it moveable. Peter Zweig and Bruce Webb, who with Sally Woodbridge and myself have been assembling this exhibition, have developed these vernacular commandments.

opposite, left, top
House, Pecos River, New Mexico
left, bottom
House, Marshall, Michigan, ca 1883
right, top
House, Waxahatchie, Texas
right, bottom
Henri Castro house, Castroville, Texas

left
Doorway, Castroville, Texas
above
Elephant Saloon, Fredricksburg, Texas

**Peter Zweig and
Bruce Webb**

THE THREE COMMAND-MENTS

*of
Vernacular
Architecture*

The First Commandment: Make it Shelter — Houses of Necessity.
The first commandment has to do with the building itself, not yet a metaphorical creation, but something content to have been built well and to work well. In this category , there are several admonitions or mandates. First, there is the matter of enclosing space: ***Make it Habitable***. Here, the concern is with how the medium of wood, stone, brick, or metal of a certain size and shape can be worked to make sheltered spaces. Whether walls and roof are woven, molded, constructed, or hollowed out, the builder begins conservatively, with trial and error and with the knowledge of how someone down the road had built his house. Professional builders have usually worked in the same way, making things the way they have seen them made before. So without formulas and equations to predict the performance of new solutions, buildings of a certain time and place often have a lot in common.

A second admonition, ***Make it Fit***, has to do with creating a building that achieves a sense of correctness with the climate and the lay of the land. While local materials strongly influenced the forms of early regional buildings, many of their distinguishing architectural features were the result of adaptations and innovations that helped to

above
*House, Pecos River,
New Mexico*
right
*Fort Parker, near
Groesbeck, Texas*

left
House, Fredricksburg,
Texas
below
House from the Sears,
Roebuck and Company
Catalogue,
Castroville, Texas

ameliorate the harsh conditions of local climates: the Texas dogtrot house had its modular pens (rooms) separated by a breezeway; in the hot, humid Gulf Coast region, awnings, shutters, and broad porches shaded oversize, breeze-facing windows; in the arid Southwest, massive masonry walls held the sun's heat against the cold nights; and the northerner's cozy house wrapped itself around a central fireplace under a steep, snow-shedding roof, muffled against the cold winter winds. Today these same techniques form the basis for contemporary, passive-energy architecture. Making it fit also means learning how to build into the California foothills and on the sandy soils of the seacoast. It means choosing the right location and then placing the house securely so that it commands views and respect, keeps out icy winter winds and welcomes pleasant summer breezes, advoids hot summer sun

but lets in warming winter sun, and knows what to hide, what to hide from, and what to make visible.

Make it Neat, our third cautionary dictum, is involved with a refinement of details and assembly, which usually indicate a pride in craftsmanship and create a feeling of permanence. Many of the embellishments on early vernacular buildings grew out of techniques for making them neat, particularly those that dealt with how one piece of construction material meets another or how its edges are hidden and protected. These various forms of refinement show up most prominently in the upright pieces of a building, especially in porch columns, door and window frames, and the barge boards and other ornaments around the eaves. Neatness offers a sense of control over the medium and usually reveals a faith in the future; it becomes a symbol of order prevailing over chaos. Before the age

of mass-production, the presence of details was a signature that indicated the hand or the builder, that a poetic consciousness had been at work, trascending the technical solutions.

The Second Commantment: Make it Look Like Something — Houses of Fancies. Most houses, however, did not stop with our first set of imperatives. By the time someone had spent the time and money to build a house that was well-formed, well-fitted, and well-made, he was not likely to let it go at that. It seemed important that the building say what kind of house its owners wanted it to be. And so, in the second realm of our commandments, that of fancies and wishes, the collecting game becomes more interesting as buildings are made over to speak about hopes and aspirations, symbolic fancies, trimmings, trends, cosmetics, and dressing up. During the later part of the nineteenth century, the Amer

ican landscape blossomed with upright little buildings, each one contribution its personality to the general clamor. Henry james, traveling through the wilds of America in 1904, likened to the monotonous rumble of his Pullman train to a landscape that seemed to be forever saying: "See what I'm making of all this — see what I'm making, see what I'm making." What was being made had much less to do with the geography of a particular place than with where its inhabitants came from and what they had seen, The little houses fastened their collections of memories and dreams onto frameworks of necessity; they reached for respect and nobility in a kind of shriveled classical revivalism, or for poetic fancy in the Queen Anne and the Carpenter Gothic, or for pastoral smugness in the country cottage. They recalled the country houses of England or how the roofs were shaped and the walls were

decorated in the buildings of Alsace or rural Virginia. In the hands of local craftsmen, styles were freely interpreted, crossbred, and then transformed by native materials.

As information and training improved, styles became codified into forms of ritualistic behavior. Standardization began to shape this behavior so that in our own century the housing industry took some of the romance out of vernacular architecture by creating endless acres of similar three-bedroom houses, each with an exterior decor that alluded to a richer historical style. Decorative elements, which have formed the primary symbolic characteristics of historical styles, have frequently evolved from the mechanics of construction and from local adaptation. They were symbols of solutions. Detached from their former function, they became a list of options for the domestic dream: Colonial, Spanish, or Tudor.

above and right
Houses, Fredricksburg, Texas
opposite
Airstream trailer, Goleta, California

Or a homebuyer could save the price of a decor package altogether by selecting Contemporary. Technology, particularly in regard to heating and cooling equipment, and the standardization of building materials and techniques took care of the basic problems of construction, adaptation, and refinement. This meant that if a builder were willing to pay the costs, he could build anything anywhere. The twentieth century landscape became a media event of manufactured dreams where one place came to look more and more like every other.

The Third Commandment: Make it a Dream — Houses of Fantasy.

Our third commandment is concerned with the realm of fantasies, which might be thought of as more elaborately sustained dreams. Fantasies create symbols in a building in much the same way that a story line propels the characters in a novel. The history of architecture is well-seasoned with the odd and the quirky, from Xanadu and the atmospheric theatre, to pleasure palaces that move along rivers, to Disneyland and Las Vegas — all of them stage sets for fantasy. What we dream as children becomes the stuff of our adult fantasies. Architectural fantasies usually have to do with size and scale and sometimes shape, while literary fantasies about architecture deal with point of view. Architectures of fantasy create a home for the imagination.

Our first fantasy buildings begin with the dollhouse, so our first mandate is to **Make it Small**. The little house is a pretty image, associated often with a gathering of precious things, the first house, perhaps, of newlyweds; it is manageable and understandable, miniaturized, and innocent as a toy. Motel cabins of the 1940s and the Texas Sunday houses used by ranchers for their weekends in town were both contracted worlds, symbolic replicas of a much larger original. The inno-

cent charm of the little house is in contrast to the breathtaking scale of the big house, whose size and presence are the only appropriate setting for Gothic tales. Big houses are often formed of many little ones, each one a place of possibilities; and sometimes a big house achieves a singular nobility and becomes, like the enormous log hotel at Old Faithful, a stretching out of possibilities. With its log construction, the Old Faithful lodge seems warm and friendly, a deliberate recollection of little cabins in the woods, even though it is so big that its lobby stirs up feelings of childhood when everything seemed a little larger. So we have another dictum, **Make it Large**, which can help us to enlarge our awareness of possibilities.

Towers punctuate the landscape and turn our gaze upward. **Make it Tall** helps us to orient ourselves and to call attention to our buildings, but the tower satisfies a more fundamental need to celebrate the spiritus mundi, the axis between earth and heaven. Before the arrival of the skyscraper, towers were reserved for only the most special buildings, which became more special and more noble by standing taller and more detached from their surroundings. Roland Barthes, who has written extensively about the Eiffel Tower, describes the fantasy of the tower as "pure uselessness." Freed from functional apologies, the tower plays out its role like "a great baroque dream which touches the limits of the irrational." For Barthes, the tower represents technical achievement, the lure of making it taller, and establishes a previously unimaginable point of view. The tower fulfills a dream to see and be seen and creates a bridge between the real earth and the imagined heavens. The same message can find its way into the house, where verticality appears in attached towers or upward reaching bays that call

out the ascending levels of body, mind, and spirit, arranged in miniature; the house becomes an upright dwelling for the imagination.

Making a place usually implies immobility, so our last mandate, **Make it Move**, seems to be a case of having our cake and eating it too. However, from prefabricated houses that were shipped around the Horn to the nineteenth century houseboat and its twentieth century counterpart, the trailer, and its big brother, the mobile home, people have acted out the desire to take not just the memory of a former place, but the place itself, on a trip across the land. This particular trail of dreams has become the ultimate contracted world, a traveling road show viewed through familiar windows. The fantasy of mobility achieved a kind of high-water mark in the tongue-in-cheek proposal for a walking city presented by the British architects, Archigram: in their scheme, not only would you take your house and family along, but the butcher, the baker, your friends and enemies, your office, and everything else you were accustomed to using on a regular basis. But moving everything around with you is clumsy business: the 14-foot Regency Chateaux mobile home with symbolic hearth, sunken living room, sunken tub, and queen-size bed offers up little more than the illusion of portability. Still, moving is a fact of contemporary life, one that has spawned a huge mobile home industry and a whole catalog of highway architecture: swept back gas stations and streamlined diners speed you on your way by day and little housettes keep you warm and cozy at night, tiny destinations in a slipstream world.

CONCLUSION

The latitude of these commandments has been broadened in this country by the variety of our terrain and climate, by the particularly diverse cultural baggage that has been unloaded onto our shores, and, too, by the democratic spirit that has placed the common man and his buildings in a lop-sided and powerful majority. There is, then, a remarkably large and rich and energetic number of vernacular buildings in America, buildings that share a strong connection with the land and its breezes, its sunshine, and its rain, with the fashions of their own times, or with times and places that are far away; they were built by the earliest settlers and they are built today, by those that knew something about architectural nuances and by those that did not or did not care; they are plain and they are elaborate, they are big and small, low and tall, vertical and horizontal, fixed and moveable, permanent and temporary, academic and ad hoc; and they come with a sense of shelter, of fancy, of fantasy, and of place, as temples, as cabins, and as trailers.

It has not been our purpose, in this catalog and this series of exhibitions, to wrest with any sort of finality the prize of American vernacular architecture from the numerous other contenders. We have hoped, rather, to expand the narrow definition that even the architects and designers have given it, to include the roots, the trunk, the branches, the leaves, and, especially, the flowers, to consider the beauty of the whole, and to suggest that the prize, so revealed, is worth the having.

—P.B.

CONTRIBUTORS

John Beach is an architectural historian, designer and frequent lecturer. Mr. Beach, who resides in Berkeley, California, is presently designing and building his own home.

Peter Becker is co-author with Charles W. Moore and Regula Campbell of *Los Angeles: The City Observed* to be published by Random House in 1984. Mr. Becker lives in Los Angeles.

Jane Bledsoe is Administrative Director of the California State University, Long Beach Art Museum. She is also an instructor in the Museum Studies Certificate Program at the University.

John Chase is the author of *Exterior Decoration* and *The Sidewalk Companion to Santa Cruz Architecture*. He resides in Los Angeles.

Barbara Coffman, architect, and **Arlan Coffman**, writer, collect contruction toys and live in Santa Monica, California.

Bob Easton is the principal of Bob Easton Design Associates in Santa Barbara, California. He is co-author with Peter Nabokov of *Native American Architecture* to be published by Oxford University Press in 1984.

Carla Fantozzi is a graduate student in Museum Studies at the University of Southern California and a Museum Educator at the J. Paul Getty Museum in Los Angeles.

Dextra Frankel is the Director of the Art Gallery-Visual Arts Center at California State University, Fullerton. She is a Professor of Art at the University and a partner in LAX Design Studios, Laguna Beach, California.

David Gebhard is a Professor of Architectural History and Curator of the Architectural Drawing Archives at the University of California, Santa Barbara. Dr. Gebhard has lectured across the country and has curated exhibitions on the subject of architecture. He is the author of *Schindler* among other books and exhibition catalogs on twentieth century architecture.

Mary Ann Beach Harrel is a collector of Craftsman, Art Nouveau, Art Deco and 1950s mass produced decorative art. She has written and lectured on California castles.

Roger A. Hart is Acting Chairman of the Environmental Psychology Program at the City University of New York.

Evelyn Hitchcock is Assistant to the Dean of the Faculty and Staff at California State University, Dominguez Hills. She will be completing her Master of Arts in architectural history during the winter of 1984.

Gere Kavanaugh is a graphic and architectural interior designer. She designs textiles with her own Geraldine Fabrics Company, curates exhibitions and is an architectural color consultant. Ms. Kavanaugh is restoring her home in the historic Angelino Heights section of Los Angeles.

Esther McCoy is an architectural historian and the author of many

142

books on California architecture including *Five California Architects*. She has written numerous articles, lectured, taught and curated exhibitions on architecture and architects.

Charles W. Moore is an architect and a Professor of Architecture at the University of California, Los Angeles. He is a former head of the architectural programs at Yale and UCLA, a partner in the firm of Moore, Grover, Harper in Essex, Connecticut and a principal of the Urban Innovations Group and the firm of Moore, Ruble, Yudell in Los Angeles. He is co-author of *The Place of Houses* among other books.

Kirk Peterson is an architect practicing in Oakland, California. His work includes historic preservation and contemporary design.

Davida Rochlin is an architect who wrote her Master of Architecture thesis at the University of California, Berkeley on the American porch. Ms Rochlin has worked in Georgia and is now with a Los Angeles firm.

Roger P. Scharmer is a consultant in landscape architecture, history, architectural preservation and city planning. He teaches at the University of California, Berkeley and the University of California, Davis Extension. Mr. Scharmer lives in Mill Valley, California,

Kathryn Smith is an architectural historian who teaches at Otis Art Institute of Parsons School of Design in Los Angeles. She is completing a forthcoming monograph entitled *Olive Hill: Frank LLoyd Wright's Designs for Aline Barnsdall.*

James Volkert is Curator of the Junior Arts Center, a Division of the Cultural Affairs Department, City of Los Angeles and an independent exhibition designer.

Nancy Walsh is the Gallery Education Coordinator at the Junior Arts Center. She lives in Los Angeles.

Bruce Webb is an Associate Professor of Architecture and the Director of Graduate Studies in Architecture at the University of Houston.

Robert Winter is a Professor of the History of Ideas at Occidental College, the author of *The California Bungalow* and co-author of *A Guide to Architecture in Los Angeles and Southern California* with David Gebhard. Dr. Winter lives in the Ernest Batchelder house, a Craftsman bungalow designed by Ernest Batchelder in Pasadena, California.

Peter Zweig is an architect and an Associate Professor of Architecture at the University of Houston.

EXHIBITIONS

*October 1983 -
June 1984*

144

The Front Porch
Craft and Folk Art Museum
October 19 - January 8
Davida Rochlin, Curator

Added-On—Ornament
University Art Museum, California State University, Long Beach
October 18 - November 13
Jane Bledsoe, Curator

The House That Art Built
Art Gallery-Visual Art Center,
California State University,
Fullerton
October 28 - December 7
Dextra Frankel, Curator

**Building by the Little Folks:
Early Architectural
Construction Toys**
Pacific Design Center
November 1 - December 30
and
The Fine Arts Gallery, University
of California, Irvine
May 8 - June 2
Arlan and Barbara Coffman,
Curators

Shadows on the Land: Dwellings in American Indian Life
Southwest Museum
November 1 - January 8
Peter Welsh, Curator

Temple-Cabin-Trailer
Los Angeles Institute of Contemporary Art
November 5 - December 23
Charles W. Moore, Curator

Hearst Castle: An Architectural Fantasy
Fisher Gallery, University of
Southern California
November 7 - December 10
Carla Fantozzi, Curator

Plank House Architecture of the Northwest Coast Indians
ARCO Center for Visual Art
November 8 - December 24
Bob Easton, Curator

Rough Housing
Junior Arts Center Gallery,
Barnsdall Park
November 8 - January 8
James Volkert, Curator

Eclectic Stucco
Architecture Gallery, Southern
California Institute of
Architecture
November 8 - November 22
Kirk Peterson, Curator

**The Common American
Bungalow** and
**Tile, Stucco Walls and Arches:
The Spanish Tradition in the
Popular American House**
Baxter Art Gallery, California
Institute of Technology
November 11 - December 11
Robert Winter, Curator
David Gebhard, Curator

The California Ranch House
University Art Gallery, California
State University, Dominguez Hills
January 5 - January 31
Esther McCoy and
Evelyn Hitchcock, Curators

Key

b – bottom
c – center
i – insert
l – left
r – right
t – top

CREDITS / SOURCES

2		Courtesy Tom and Holly Delach
3		Max King
6		M. Witmark & Sons, New York, 1920.
9		Courtesy Lauren M. Kasmer
10		Courtesy Sally Cullman, Lauren M. Kasmer, Max King, Susan Skinner
14		Courtesy Lauren M. Kasmer, Max King, Susan Skinner, David Weiss
18		Courtesy Fred Rochlin
	i	Courtesy American-Standard Inc.
22		Brenda Hurst
23	*tl*	Blaine Mallory
	bl	Michael Webb
	r	Max King
24		Courtesy Library of Congress, Washington, D.C.
25	*tl*	Courtesy Georgia Department of Archives and History
	bl	Courtesy Atlanta Historical Society
	r	Courtesy Sears, Roebuck and Company
26	*l*	Davida Rochlin
	cr	John Carleton
	tr	Courtesy Chatillon-DeMenil House
	br	Courtesy Chatillon-DeMenil House
27	*bl*	Courtesy Atlanta Historical Society
	t	H.Hess—McMillan Company, Publishers
	br	*Style in Home Furnishing*
28		Davida Rochlin
29		Davida Rochlin
30	*l*	Karen Safer-Polich
	r	Courtesy Hartmann-Sanders Company
31	*l*	Karen Safer-Polich
	br	Lauren M. Kasmer
	cr	Edwards Manufacturing Company, Cincinnati
	tr	Max King
32	*tl*	Max King
	tr	Max King
	b	Karen Safer-Polich
33	*t*	Karen Safer-Polich
	bl	Edgar and Verna Cook Salomonsky—Boston Varnish Company
	br	Lauren M. Kasmer
34	*tl*	Max King
	tr	Karen Safer-Polich
	b	William S. Comstock, New York
35	*l*	Brenda Hurst
	ct	Blaine Mallory
	cb	Brenda Hurst
	r	Blaine Mallory
36	*tl*	Folke Nyberg
	bl	Michael Webb
	tr	Max King
	br	Max King
37	*l*	Max King
	cl,	Max King
	cr	Blaine Mallory
	r	Max King
38		Max King

145

b   Courtesy Cliff May-L.J. Geddes, photographer

84   Evelyn Hitchcock

85 *l*   Courtesy California Historical Society-Ticor Title Insurance, Los Angeles

    tr   R.W. Brackett, *A History of the Ranchos of San Diego County, California*, Ticor Title Insurance, Los Angeles

    br   Courtesy California State University, Dominguez Hills, Rancho San Pedro and Dominguez Family Papers

86 *tl*   *Historic American Buildings Survey 45, California Volume I*

    bl   R.W. Brackett, *A History of the Ranchos of San Diego County, California*, Ticor Title Insurance, Los Angeles

    br   Courtesy California Historical Society, Ticor Title Insurance, Los Angeles

87 *l*   *Historic American Buildings Survey 45, California Volume I*

    t   R.W. Brackett, *A History of the Ranchos of San Diego County, California*, Ticor Title Insurance, Los Angeles

    r   Courtesy Southwest Museum

88   Courtesy California Historical Society, Ticor Title Insurance, Los Angeles

89   Courtesy Cliff May

90   Michael Webb

91 *l*   Ted Brown Music Company, Chicago

    r   Courtesy American Museum of Natural History, New York

92   Courtesy Smithsonian Institution National Anthropological Archives, Washington, D.C.

93   Courtesy Smithsonian Institution National Anthropological Archives, Washington, D.C.

94 *l*   Denver Art Museum

    tr   Courtesy American Museum of Natural History, New York

    br   Courtesy Smithsonian Institution National Anthropological Archives, Washington, D.C.

95 *tl*   Courtesy Library of Congress, Washington, D.C.

    bl   Courtesy British Columbia Provincial Museum, Victoria, British Columbia

    tr   Courtesy Smithsonian Institution National Anthropological Archives, Washington, D.C.

    br   Courtesy Smithsonian Institution National Anthropological Archives,

96 *l*   Courtesy British Columbia Provincial Museum, Victoria, British Columbia

    r   Courtesy National Museums of Canada, Ottawa

97   Courtesy British Columbia Provincial Museum, Victoria, British Columbia

98 *t*   Thacker, Spink and Company, Calcutta, India

    b   Courtesy Robert Winter

99   William S. Comstock, New York

100   Southern Cypress Manufacturers Association, New Orleans

101 *l*   Henry S. Wilson, Chicago

    r   The Radford Architectural Company, Chicago

102   Dixi Carrillo

103 *tl*   Pacific Ready-Cut Homes, Los Angeles

    bl   Kirk Peterson

    r   John Chase

104   Pacific Ready-Cut Homes, Los Angeles

105 *l*   Crane Company, Chicago

    r   Gustav Stickley, *Craftsman House*, New York

106   Shrewsbury Publishing Company, Chicago

107   *Sunset Magazine*, San Francisco

108 *l*   *The Minneapolis Tribune*, Minneapolis

    tr   Ye Planary Company, Los Angeles

    br   Home Owners Service Institute, New York

109 *t*   Bank of America, San Francisco

    b   The Bungalowcrafts Company, Los Angeles

110   California Develoment Corporation- Samona, Inc.

111   Max King

112 *l*   Kirk Peterson

    r   Dixi Carrillo

113   Dixi Carrillo

114   Dixi Carrillo

115   Kirk Peterson

116   Kirk Peterson

117   Kirk Peterson

118   Lauren M. Kasmer

119 *tl*   Lauren M. Kasmer

    tc   Max King

    tr   Lauren M. Kasmer

    b   Lauren M. Kasmer

120 *l*   Lauren M. Kasmer

    c   Max King

    r   Lauren M. Kasmer

121 *tl*   Lauren M. Kasme

    bl   Max King

    cl   Lauren M. Kasmer

    cr   John Chase

    r   Lauren M. Kasmer

122   Lauren M. Kasmer

123 *l*   Lauren M. Kasmer

    c   Max King

    r   Max King

124 *l*   Lauren M. Kasmer

    tcl   Max King

    bcl   Lauren M. Kasmer

    tcr   Max King

    bcr   Lauren M. Kasmer

    tr   Lauren M. Kasmer

125   Lauren M. Kasmer

126   Lauren M. Kasmer

127 *l*   Max King

    r   Lauren M. Kasmer

128   Lauren M. Kasmer

129 *l*   Max King

    r   Lauren M. Kasmer

130   Sherman, Clay and Company, San Francisco

131 *b*   Courtesy©1946, Walt Disney Productions

132 *t*   Courtesy David Weiss

    bl   Carl Miller

    br   Courtesy Lauren M. Kasmer

133 *bl*   Max King

    br   Blaine Mallory

    tr   Charles W. Moore

    br   Betty Bollinger

134 *tl*   Charles W. Moore

    bl   Charles W. Moore

    tr   Carl Miller

    br   Carl Miller

135   Carl Miller

136 *t*   Charles W. Moore

    b   Carl Miller

137   Carl Miller

138   Carl Miller

139   Max King

140   Courtesy Lauren M Kasmer, Max King, Susan Skinner, David Weiss

144   Thea Delaportas

The Craft and Folk Art Museum of Los Angeles, founded in 1973, has established programs of collection, publication, education and conservation in crafts, design, architecture, popular culture, folk art and ethnic traditions. In addition to hosting traditional museum activities, the Craft and Folk Art Museum emphasizes cooperative programming among regional, cultural and educational institutions.

CRAFT AND FOLK ART MUSEUM

PRODUCTION NOTES

Edition
4,000 copies

Paper
Lustro Offset Enamel

Typography
Text—Rockwell
Headline—Avant Garde

Project Coordinator
Blaine Mallory

Editors
Charles W. Moore
Kathryn Smith
Peter Becker

Readers
Marcia Page
Joan Benedetti

Designer/Creative Director
Max King

Assistant to M. King/B. Mallory
Lauren M. Kasmer

Photography
see Credits/Sources section

Print Production
Grunfeld and Brandt

Additional Production Services
Focus Foto Finishers
Roberts Negative & Stripping
Stat House
Tin Roof Typography

Cover Design
Gere Kavanaugh
Max King

Cover Illustrations
Charles W. Moore

Cover Photograph
Oscar Castillo
Mike Sasso